AROUND toronto WITH KIDS

by Kate Pocock

Fodor's Travel Publications
New York • Toronto • London • Sydney • Auckland

www.fodors.com

CREDITS
Writer: Kate Pocock

Series Editor: Karen Cure
Editor: Christina Knight
Editorial Production: Tom Holton
Production/Manufacturing: Angela L. McLean

Design: Fabrizio La Rocca, *creative director*;
Tigist Getachew, *art director*
Illustration and Series Design: Rico Lins, Keren Ora
Admoni/Rico Lins Studio

ABOUT THE WRITER
Since November 1994, Kate Pocock has written a family travel column for the *Toronto Sun*, Family Fare, as well as articles for numerous magazines and Internet sites. She is Senior Editor of *Travel & More* magazine for the Canadian Air Miles program and was a contributor to *the National Geographic Guide to Family Adventure Vacations*. For her writing, she has won a Parenting Publication of America award and a Baseball Writers of America award. She lives in the Beaches neighborhood of Toronto with her husband and three children.

ISBN 0-679-00723-7
ISSN 1533-5291
First Edition

Important Tip
Although all prices, opening times, and other details in this book are based on information supplied to us at press time, changes occur all the time in the travel world, and Fodor's cannot accept responsibility for facts that become outdated or for inadvertent errors or omissions. So always confirm information when it matters, especially if you're making a detour to visit a specific place.

Special Sales
Fodor's Travel Publications are available at special discounts for bulk purchases for sales promotions or premiums. Special editions, including personalized covers, excerpts of existing guides, and corporate imprints, can be created in large quantities for special needs. For more information, contact your local bookseller or Special Markets, Fodor's Travel Publications, 280 Park Avenue, New York, NY 10017. Inquiries from Canada should be directed to your local Canadian bookseller or sent to Random House of Canada, Ltd., Marketing Dept., 2775 Matheson Boulevard East, Mississauga, Ontario L4W 4P7. Inquiries from the United Kingdom should be sent to Fodor's Travel Publications, 20 Vauxhall Bridge Road, London, England SW1V 2SA.

PRINTED IN THE UNITED STATES OF AMERICA
10 9 8 7 6 5 4 3 2 1

COUNTDOWN TO GOOD TIMES

GET READY, GET SET!

E veryone knows that organizing a family's schedule is a full-time job. Pickups, drop-offs, school, parties, after-school activities—everyone off in their own direction. Of course, it's an organizer's dream, but a scheduling nightmare. Spending time together shouldn't be another thing to have to figure out.

We know what's it's like to try to find good places to take your children or grandchildren. Sometimes it's tough to change plans when you suddenly hear about a kid-friendly event; besides, a lot of those events end up being crowded or, worse, sold out. It's also hard to remember places you read about in a newspaper or magazine, and sometimes just as hard to tell from the description what age group they're geared to. There's nothing like bringing a "grown-up" 12-year-old to an activity that's intended for his 6-year-old sister. Of course, if you're visiting Toronto, it's even harder to figure out the best things to do with your kids before you even get there. That's where we come in.

What you'll find in this book are 68 ways to have a terrific couple of hours or an entire day with children in tow. Downtown Toronto is full of world-class attractions, cultural events, and creative, urban architecture yet is only minutes from bike paths, birdwatching sites, and the shores of Lake Ontario. We've scoured the city, digging out activities your kids will love—from the shores of Lake Ontario to the streetscapes of Chinatown and St. Lawrence Market. The best part is that it's stress-free, uncomplicated, and easy for you. Open the book to any page and find a helpful description of a kid-friendly attraction, with age ratings to make sure it's right for your family, smart tips on visiting so that you can get the most out of your time there, and family-friendly eats nearby. The address, telephone number, open hours, and admission prices are all there for your convenience. We've done the work, so you don't have to.

The free monthly *City Parent* newspaper (www.cityparent.com) lists dozens of current activities around town. You'll find it at most large bookstores and some toy stores, banks, libraries, supermarkets, and family attractions. Thursday's *Toronto Star* has a rundown of most weekend events, and includes a section for kids. Also, read the calendar in the monthly *Toronto Life* magazine for theatre listings and special events for families.

WAYS TO SAVE MONEY

We list only regular adult, student (with I.D.), and kids' prices; children under the ages specified are free. It always pays to ask at the ticket booth whether any discounts are offered for a particular status or affiliation (but don't forget to bring your I.D.). Discounts are often available for senior citizens, and CAA and AAA members, among others. Many places offer family entrance fees, or memberships, generally good for one year of unlimited use. These memberships sometimes allow you to bring a guest. Prices vary, but the memberships often pay for themselves if you visit the attraction several times a year. Sometimes there are other perks: newsletters or magazines, members-only previews, and discounts at a gift shop, for parking, or for birthday parties or special events. If you like a place when you visit, you can sometimes apply the value of your one-day admission to a membership if you do it before you leave.

Also keep an eye out for attractions—mostly museums and other cultural destinations—that offer free admission one day a month or one day a week after a certain time. We've noted several in this book.

WHEN TO GO

With the exception of seasonal attractions, kid-oriented destinations are generally the most crowded when children are out of school—especially weekends, holidays, and summer— but not necessarily. The busiest school break is the second week of March (at some schools, the third week), and attractions often put on special events during this time. Museums that draw school trips can be swamped with clusters of children tall enough to block the view of your preschooler. But school groups tend to leave by early afternoon, so weekdays after 2 during the school year can be an excellent time to visit museums and zoos.

The hours we list are the basic hours, not necessarily those applicable on holidays. Some attractions are closed when schools are closed, but others add extra hours on these days. It's always best to check if you want to see an attraction on a holiday.

VISITING TORONTO

Prices in this book are listed in Canadian dollars, and according to Canadian usage, words adhere to British spellings (as in "colour"). Take note of the national holidays: The Friday before and Monday after Easter; Victoria Day (third Monday in May); Canada Day (July 1); Civic Holiday Day (also known as Bank Holiday or Simcoe Day; first Monday in August); Labour Day (first Monday in September), after which school starts on Tuesday; Thanksgiving (second Monday in October); Remembrance Day (November 11), Christmas, and Boxing Day (December 26).

SAFETY

Obviously the amount of vigilance necessary will depend on the attraction and the ages of your kids. In crowded attractions, keep an eye on your children at all times, as their ages warrant. When you arrive, point out what the staff or security people are wearing, and find a very visible landmark to use as a meeting place, should you get separated. If you do split into groups, pick a time to meet. This will decrease waiting time, help you and your kids get the most out of your time there, and manage everyone's expectations.

FINAL THOUGHTS

Actually, this time it's yours, not ours. We'd love to hear what you or your kids thought about the attractions you visited. Or if you happened upon a place that you think warrants inclusion, by all means, send it along, so the next family can enjoy Toronto even more. You can e-mail us at editors@fodors.com (specify Around Toronto With Kids on the subject line), or write to us at Fodor's Around Toronto with Kids, 280 Park Avenue, New York, NY 10017. We'll put your ideas to good use. In the meantime, have fun!

THE EDITORS

AFRICAN LION SAFARI

How often do you get to be the "animal" in the cage? At African Lion Safari just west of Toronto, lions, tigers, and giraffes roam freely while families view them from the safety of their cars. You can't always predict if creatures will run to greet you (and you may not want them to). But as you wind your way along the 10-km (6-mi) trail, you'll get close enough to count wrinkles or teeth. You may even have your car window licked by a llama or used as a slide by baboons, a highlight for the kids.

Canada's largest safari park opened more than 30 years ago with 40 lions (the ads advised against convertibles) and a mission to promote conservation. Today, you can visit with 1,000 birds and animals and 132 species from Africa, Asia, and North America. You'll see glimpses of baby Asian elephants—seven have been born at the park—and watch rare hawks or eagles at the Birds of Prey Conservation Centre, the largest collection in North America. Any new baby, from a South African white rhino to a Newfoundland pony to a barn owl, is a cause for celebration.

HEY, KIDS! It's big news when a baby elephant is born here, and that's not just because it weighs over 200 pounds! The Asian elephant is an endangered species that gets special attention at this safari. How do they like the Canadian winter? They sleep in a large heated barn and have their baths indoors, just like you. On warm days, they go outside to play, just like you. How do they drink? They suck water up through their noses and squirt it into their mouths—not like you at all!

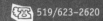 Safari Rd.

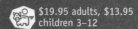 $19.95 adults, $13.95 children 3–12

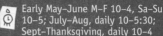 Early May–June M–F 10–4, Sa–Su 10–5; July–Aug, daily 10–5:30; Sept–Thanksgiving, daily 10–4

519/623–2620

 All ages

Plan to spend a good day here. Your kids can handle ostrich eggs at the Discovery Centre, pet a goat in the Pets' Corner, and watch eagles perform at a Birds of Prey show. There are pony and bareback elephant rides, cruises aboard the *African Queen*, rides on the scenic railway, and water play for kids and elephants—kids can splash down at the interactive Misumu Bay Wet Play while the elephants dowse themselves during daily Elephant Swims in the lake nearby.

But the biggest thrill is driving through the seven fenced game reserves populated by bison, yaks, zebras, and stunning white tigers. Most hilarious are the baboons who leap onto cars to ride sidesaddle on the side-view mirrors, swing on car aerials, or slide down the front windows. This memorable monkey business is a hoot.

GETTING THERE The park is about 25 minutes from the city limits. Take the Gardiner Expressway to Queen Elizabeth Way (QEW) westbound, then take Highway 403 west toward Hamilton. At Highway 6, drive north towards Guelph. Turn west at Safari Road. Or take Highway 401 to the Highway 8 cutoff. Go south to Safari Road, turn east, and follow the signs.

KEEP IN MIND Curious baboons may cause damage to vehicles as they bend aerials, steal light bulbs from license plates, or try to pry open a sun roof or window. Kids love it, so be prepared to linger a while on the Wankie Bushland Trail. If you don't want to subject your own transportation to these playful pranks, hitch a ride on the Safari Tour Bus ($4.95 adults, $4.45 children 3–12; free for moms on Mother's Day). But it's not nearly as much fun and sticks to its one-hour and 15 minute schedule.

T alk about quick-change artists! At the Air Canada Centre arena, the floor is in constant flux, switching from ice for the Toronto Maple Leafs hockey team to a basketball court for the Toronto Raptors to Astroturf for the Toronto lacrosse team, The Rock. The surface has even been covered with mounds of snow for the Canadian Super Snowcross, the first-ever indoor snowmobile races in a snow-sculpted setting. But then, the building itself is a bit of a chameleon. What was built as the city's Art Deco Postal Delivery Building in 1939 has been transformed into a razzmatazz entertainment venue for concerts, family shows such as *Disney on Ice*, WWF Wrestling, and other professional sporting events.

If the home teams are not in town, the one-hour guided tour will give you a good behind-the-scenes look at the dressing rooms, as well as the Raptors' impressive practice court, and the kinds of suites that would set you back a cool $260,000 a year, such as Leaf tough guy Tie Domi's. In the Esso Maple Leaf Memories & Dreams room (open always

HEY, KIDS!

You can check out the TD Waterhouse Fan Zone at Gate 1, open for two hours before every hockey or basketball game. Have your picture taken with a famous sports cutout, shoot a puck or some baskets, and try interactive games and quizzes. It's free!

EATS FOR KIDS There's a fast-food court off the Galleria, open during events, that sells pizza, hot dogs, or doughnuts. If you're feeling flush, however, take your older kids to the **Air Canada Club** (tel. 416/815–5983), which overlooks the bowl and gets rave ratings for its cuisine. Nearby, the **Hot House Café** (35 Church, tel. 416/366–7800) greets kids with colouring books and crayons. Its kids' menu for 10 and unders offers kiddie portions with pop (soda) and ice cream for only $3.79. Another good choice: **Shopsy's** (33 Yonge St., tel. 416/365–3333) with its huge menu, deli sandwiches, soup, and famous dogs.

40 Bay St.

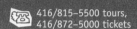 416/815–5500 tours,
416/872–5000 tickets

 Tours $9.50 adults,
$7.50 students 13 and up,
$6.50 children 12 and
under. Events vary

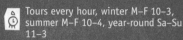 Tours every hour, winter M–F 10–3,
summer M–F 10–4, year-round Sa–Su
11–3

 7 and up

during games), you'll see photos and artifacts of Toronto's beloved Maple Leafs players since the early days. Don't forget the camera to click a pix of your kids in goalie Curtis Joseph's equipment. One of the funniest up-close encounters in the building is with a Raptor's Nike shoe that's handed around—at size 18, it's as long as child's arm.

Of course, the real action is in the stands, where you'll be able to see the details even from the back-row seats. The sightlines are terrific. The Big Screen ensures that you don't miss any plays. During a season's 41 home basketball games, you'll be entertained by contests, games, circus acts, dancing cheerleaders, and of course, The Raptor doing tricks on the trampoline or shooting golf balls into the crowd. It's fast, fun, and ferocious! The hockey games attract an older crowd but are always packed with enthusiastic spectators. Hockey lovers pass down their season tickets to their children or leave them in their wills.

KEEP IN MIND The Air Canada Centre was created with families in mind. There are baby changing tables and small urinals in the washrooms; concession counters are low so kids can order their own drinks. The basketball games begin at 7 PM so kids can be tucked into bed early. On a strict budget? Ask about the Family Four Pack basketball tickets that give four seats, hot dogs, and drinks; the $10.50 Sprite Zone that entertains kids with contests, giveaways, or face painting; or, the less expensive Coke Zone tickets set aside each month for hockey games.

ALLAN GARDENS CONSERVATORY

Where better to shed the greyness of a Toronto winter than in the Allan Gardens Conservatory? Once inside this steamy, jungle atmosphere in the middle of a downtown city park, snowsuits and jackets can be peeled away. Mittens too—all the better to touch the palm fronds or feel the shiny leaves of a hens and chickens plant as you walk the stone paths under jungle greenery. Five display houses exhibit cacti, tropical plants, palm trees, vines, and lush exotics from Australia, the Caribbean, Africa, and other hot spots. Within minutes, you're in a tropical world far removed from downtown Toronto.

Toddlers seem to love this historic conservatory, built in 1910 as a large palm house with adjoining glass wings. Trees tower above them and even the cacti in the Arid House are taller than mom and dad. It's also a sensory experience. Water drips from a waterwheel into a pond, scents from tropical fruit trees or blooming hyacinths float through the air, goldfish flit about, and light pours down through the 18-m (60-ft) dome. Your teens may

HEY, KIDS! The greenhouse staff doesn't use chemicals or pesticides to control pesky insects. Instead, they use other insects to destroy creatures that might harm the plants. For example, lacewings are good at eating harmful aphids or whitefly. An Australian lady beetle will feed on mealybugs. See if you can spot any of these tiny warriors in the plants or walking along the stone paths. Be careful not to step on any small insects. A little, bitty bug with waving feelers could be a powerful helper in the greenhouse.

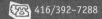 19 Horticultural Ave.

 416/392-7288

  Free

 M–F 9–4, Sa–Su and holidays 10–5

All ages

not be so enamored with discovering a palm from Madagascar or a miniature holly bush from the West Indies. But why not bring along a sketch book or a camera? No permits are necessary to capture the unusual shapes or colours on paper or on film.

The Conservatory really comes alive at Christmastime, when red poinsettias decorate every room and late afternoon candlelight casts a glow on the homemade wreaths and garlands. On the opening day of the Victorian flower show, the first Sunday of December, you can ride a horse and buggy in the surrounding 13-acre park, sip apple cider, and make holiday decorations. Every season brings new surprises—from flowering bulbs in the spring to moist heat in summer and rich colour in the fall. With over 16,000 sq ft of display space, it's an urban oasis of light, colour, and warmth.

KEEP IN MIND
Because Allan Gardens is an inner city park close to home-less shelters, some transients use this park as a resting spot during the day. It's also a favourite for dogwalkers. Though police patrol regularly, it's unwise to let young children roam the grounds on their own.

EATS FOR KIDS In the same building on the corner of Gerrard and Jarvis, try **Church's Chicken** or **Harvey's** (278 Jarvis St., tel. 416/977–4583) for fried chicken or hamburgers. At Ryerson Polytechnical University down Gerrard Street, you'll find reasonably priced fare at hot dog carts and student cafeterias. Fill up at **Young Thailand** (111 Gerrard St. E., tel. 416/599–9099) with an all-you-can-eat lunch buffet for $7.95. Of course, you can picnic among the flowers outside the Conservatory on one of the many park benches, or by the fountain on the west side of the greenhouse, where there's a small playground.

ART GALLERY OF ONTARIO

Whether sculpting their mashed potatoes, or doodling in their notebooks, kids have creativity to burn. The Art Gallery of Ontario is just the place to channel that enthusiasm. At the activity centre, workshops, Family Sundays (with live children's entertainment on the first Sunday of every month), and art-inspired birthday parties (*see* Keep in Mind), kids can express themselves in paint and pastels, clay and colour, and develop a lifelong appreciation of fine art. Your budding artist can browse the collection for inspiration—the 24,000 works include Inuit carvings, Old Master portraits, Group of Seven landscapes, and bizarre contemporary works that kids can often interpret as convincingly as any curator.

Three main events on Family Sundays keep the gallery hopping: the Off the Wall! Dr. Mariano Elia Hands-On Centre, workshops for kids ages 3–10 and their parents, and Family Fun in the Galleries where you might find Dutch costumes in the Dutch gallery or Inuit sculpting materials in the Inuit area. The most popular activities in the Off the Wall! Centre is

KEEP IN MIND

The AGO hosts birthday parties with themes such as Puppet Parties, ages 4–6, Magical Wizardry for ages 7–10, or a "Back to the Future" party, ages 8–12. Cost for stories, tours, and art materials is $22 per child (10–15 guests).

EATS FOR KIDS

Skip the elegant skylit gallery restaurant, agora, and opt instead for the cheerful **Cultures Market** cafeteria (tel. 416/593–9647) with its pizza, pasta, salads, famous fruit smoothies, and homemade cookies. In summer, kids can people-watch or pigeon-chase on the outdoor patio. Chinatown restaurants are minutes away or you can picnic behind the gallery in Grange Park where there are tables and a small playground. Teens should enjoy a meal on funky Baldwin Street (two blocks north just west of McCaul). The casual **Café La Gaffe** (24 Baldwin St., tel. 416/596–2397) serves bistro fare and plays jazz music over the sound system.

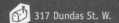
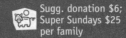

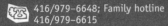

"magic lantern," where kids project their coloured slide drawings onto a wall, and "you're framed," where little designers fashion themselves into fairy princesses in gossamer halos, green dragons with horns, and wizards wearing silver moons. For $3, you can capture them as part of a painting on Polaroid. The excitement and noise can be too much for some, stimulating for others.

If your kids have never been here before, first visit the Gallery Shop to pick out postcards for a scavenger hunt. Set out to discover the blue-spotted trees by painter Lawren Harris in the Group of Seven gallery, the strange seated figures by sculptor Henry Moore, or the giant hamburger by Claes Oldenburg in the contemporary wing.

Don't miss the Grange, the 1817 home that served as the city's first art gallery. Here, children can taste scones in the historic kitchen, climb the grand staircase to the girls' bedrooms, and complete the activity booklet to receive a surprise.

HEY, KIDS! Want to try some artwork at home? Visit the chock-a-block art supply store just around the corner called Aboveground Art Supplies (74 McCaul St., tel. 416/591–1601 or 800/591–1615). The art students next door at the Ontario College of Art and Design shop here for the huge variety of materials at good prices. There's a special kids section on the second floor where you can find coloured markers, pastels, charcoal pencils, and watercolour kits—tons of stuff to create your own masterpieces. The store is open M–Th 8:30–7:30, F 8:30–6, Sa 10–6, and some Sundays.

ARTHUR CONAN DOYLE COLLECTION

64

Believe it or not, Toronto is home to one of the world's largest collections of Sherlock Holmes memorabilia. Take the scenic windowed elevator of the Toronto Reference Library to the fifth floor and there, hidden away, you'll find a library room that's straight out of Sir Arthur Conan Doyle's famous Victorian stories. It's as if Sherlock Holmes, fiction's greatest detective ever, had just stepped out from his sitting room at Baker Street in London, England, to solve a case. There's an Eastern throw draped over the cosy chair by the fireplace, a seltzer bottle on the mantle, a wicker basket filled with pipes over by the glass cabinet, and on a file box, school chemistry class–like bottles filled with suspect liquids, and a microscope ready to look at clues. "It's his Toronto office," teases a library assistant with a smile.

Of course, it's also a library with hundreds of books, written about or by Holmes's creator, Sir Arthur Ignatius Conan Doyle. For 43 years, Doyle, a medical doctor, wrote about the capers of Holmes and his pal Dr. Watson as they tackled the foggy streets and misty moors

KEEP IN MIND At the Lillian H. Smith branch (239 College St.), The Merril Collection of Science Fiction, Speculation, and Fantasy (tel. 416/393–7748) displays a world-renowned collection of science fiction, fantasy, and horror—everything from role-playing games and Star Wars comics to science fiction classics. An undiscovered treasure one floor up is the Osborne Collection of Early Children's Books (tel. 416/393–7753), containing children's literature from the 14th–early 20th centuries and Canadian children's books. Themed exhibits might display magic dragons, steam trains, or faeries from books through the centuries. *See* Lillian H. Smith Library Branch for details.

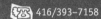 789 Yonge St.

 Free

 T, Th, Sa 2–4 or by appointment

416/393–7158

10 and up

solving mysteries. The Collection contains 5,000 volumes as well as thousands of other related items—the Persian slipper stuffed with tobacco on the mantle and a fountain pen sent by Doyle's secretary. Your kids will no doubt gravitate to the Sherlock Holmes stuffed teddy bears, the rows of Holmes figurines, and the cutout from Disney's "The Great Mouse Detective" with a pipe-smoking Bearlock Holmes.

Browse around the room as if searching for your own clues. You'll find bound copies of *The Strand Magazine* in which 56 Holmes stories were published, busts of Napoléon, original illustrations, copies of the 56 stories and four novels in 80 languages from Hungarian to Hebrew in every form from paperback to leather-bound. If you find a story that you want to share with the kids, curl up by the window or by the fireplace, or sit down on one of the leather-cushioned chairs at the library table. Kids who already know Sherlock Holmes will be entranced; those who don't will be inspired to get to know him.

HEY, KIDS! You can't take materials out of the Toronto Reference Library but if you see any Sherlock Holmes audio tapes or videos that interest you, take them to the fourth floor. The librarians there will show you where to find the tape or video players.

EATS FOR KIDS A coffee wagon in the lobby sells drinks, muffins, and chips. **The Bloor St. Diner** in the Manulife Centre (55 Bloor St. W., tel. 416/928–3105) is where preteens get a peek at French bistro ambience while munching on individual pizzas and pastas. If your kids like noodles, **The Green Mango** (730 Yonge St., tel. 416/928–0021) serves mild Thai noodle dishes like *pad thai.* **Flo's Diner** (70 Yorkville Ave., tel. 416/961–4333) hits the spot for breakfast, lunch, or dinner.

BATA SHOE MUSEUM

63

How many kids have seen the deerskin boots worn by an Apache medicine man, or tiny silk slippers once used to bind a girl's feet, or chestnut-crushing clogs with jagged spikes from the 1800s? Similarly, how many parents? But thanks to the globe-trotting endeavors of one Mrs. Sonja Bata, married to a shoe-manufacturing giant, these and dozens of other examples of rare footwear are under one roof at the Bata Shoe Museum. According to the Guinness Book of World Records, it's said to be the largest shoe collection in the world. Move over, Imelda.

Start your visit on the lower level where All About Shoes gives kids a look at how people have covered their feet through the ages. You'll learn how shoes, from ancient Egyptian wooden sandals to astronaut Alan Lovell's moon boots, were the markers of profession, status, and job description. Most popular is the small castle where View-Masters mounted into the walls show scenes from *Cinderella*. Displayed under lights in the turrets are exquisite

HEY, KIDS!

After seeing all the shoes inside the museum, be sure to look at the building from the outside. Architect Raymond Moriyama designed it to look like a shoe box. Perhaps he imagined a giant lifting up the roof lid to peek at the treasures inside.

KEEP IN MIND Admission is free the first Tuesday of every month. Once a month, the museum holds its "Just for Little Feet" Saturday afternoon workshops. Some activities are geared to all ages such as the Feast of Sinterklaas activity when youngsters paint a pair of real Dutch clogs to take home (in honor of Sinterklaas, who leaves Christmas treats in wooden shoes). Some are restricted to kids over seven such as the Sock Babies sessions. Participants transform a gym sock into a toy for a younger sibling. The $5–$10 fee includes materials and museum admission. Call ahead to register 416/979–7799, ext. 226.

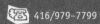
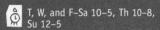
examples of what could have been the famous glass slipper. Younger children will want to linger but preteens are more impressed upstairs in the Star Turns room where Elton John's outrageous silver platforms, Ginger Spice's running shoes, or Princess Di's fuchsia pumps take centre stage. The gift shop doesn't sell shoes to wear but does offer shoe-related items— everything from a shoe-adorned umbrella to wire-woven shoes for plants.

Not all of the 10,000 shoes and related artifacts can be exhibited at one time. Hence, the constantly changing exhibits on the upper floors where families might find duck feather overshoes worn by Inuit hunters, the first ice skates or Rollerblades, or even the scuba diving fins belonging to explorer Joe Guiness, who reached the sunken *Titanic*. Of course, not all the footwear speaks of happy times as the bronzed shoes of a boy from a concentration camp will testify. But a look at the world's events through its shoes should provide for some interesting discussions.

EATS FOR KIDS Just across the street are a number of family-style restaurants. **Swiss Chalet** (234 Bloor St. W., tel. 416/972–6831), a favourite, has roast chicken or barbecued ribs with baked potatoes or fries. Or, you can brown bag it in the museum's lunch room for free. Just behind the museum is the University of Toronto campus for eating alfresco. If the weather is bad, try the Hart House cafeteria, **The Arbor Room** (7 Hart House Circle, tel. 416/978–8392) for soup, salads, and burgers.

THE BEACHES

Yes, Toronto has a beach. It's the name of a neighbourhood (called both The Beach and The Beaches), a stretch of sand, and you might say, a state of mind. For this laid-back community filled with kids and dogs hosts the kinds of events associated with simpler times—the schmaltzy Easter Parade, when the whole neighbourhood dresses in bonnets and bunny suits to walk down the main drag, and the summertime Beaches Jazz Festival, when people throng Queen Street to listen to rooftop bands or watch the dancing firemen at the local Fire Hall. This area has been a city getaway since the early 1900s. You'll no longer find amusement parks along the shore, but you can still walk the 3-km (1.8-mi) boardwalk, stop for an ice cream or a concert in the Victorian bandshell, and build castles in the sand.

As you stroll along the wooden boardwalk, with the beach on one side and the leafy park on the other, you'll pass good playgrounds for younger kids (at Silver Birch, Woodbine, and Kew Gardens), tennis courts and a roller hockey rink, and at the western end,

EATS FOR KIDS What a relief to find eateries that welcome babies and strollers. Every family has its favourite. Particularly good is **Lick's** (1960 Queen St. E., tel. 416/691–2305) for homemade burgers and tasty shakes, **The Sunset Grill** (2006 Queen St. E., tel. 416/690–9985) for all-day breakfasts that should last a week, and **Yumei Sushi** (2116 Queen St., tel. 416/698–7705) where you can sit in a Japanese booth and try chicken teriyaki. See also R.C. Harris Filtration Plant for good restaurants in the eastern section.

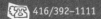

picturesque Ashbridge's Bay, with lots of sand for building moats and burying Dad. Although some parents let their kids swim here (there's a lifeguard in summer), it's not recommended due to questionable cleanliness and a slight undertow. Instead, take the gang into the free Donald Summerville Olympic Pool to test the children's pool, Olympic-size lap pool, and well-equipped diving pool. Alongside the boardwalk is the paved Waterfront Trail so if you'd like, bring your bikes.

Your too-cool teen may want to wander off to watch the beach volleyball games featuring championship players like Olympian Mark Heese who lives in the neighbourhood, or to shop at the funky stores along Queen Street. Even the family dogs are happy here. There is a swimming area for canines (east of Munro Park Avenue) and afterward, the Three Dog Bakery (2014 Queen St. E., tel. 416/693–3364) will serve up refreshments and treats at tables just for them.

HEY, KIDS! Did you know that it was in The Beach in 1908 that American pilot Charles Willard showed off the first airplane that most Torontonians had ever seen? His tragic story is in a terrific book on Toronto for kids, *The Toronto Story*, by Claire Mackay.

KEEP IN MIND Parking is scarce, so if you plan to visit on the weekend, take the #501 Queen Streetcar east and get off at either Coxwell or Woodbine avenues. From here it's a short walk to the beach. The Eastern Ravine & Beaches self-guided Discovery Walk ends at Beaches Park, so you could follow the signs and hike up into the wooded Glen Stewart Ravine. Here, you'll find fallen trees, wildflowers, and rippling Ames Creek, one of the few remaining natural streams in the city. Call tel. 416/392–1111 for a free Eastern Ravine & Beaches map.

BLACK CREEK PIONEER VILLAGE

If 21st-century household chores set your kids whining, open their eyes to "Life in the Past Line" at Black Creek Pioneer Village, where they can pitch in with period chores and—hey, are they actually enjoying the work? Following the Country Kids Trail, everyone can try their hand at carding the sheep's wool, churning the butter, dipping the candles, and braiding the rugs. The village of some 40 buildings is spread out on 56 acres, part of which was once the early 19th-century land of pig farmer Daniel Strong and his eight children. The Strongs' original log cabin still stands and the tinsmith, the clockmaker, the broommaker, and the weaver go about their daily business in their respective establishments.

Of course, there were fun and games in the old days, too. Little ones will love visiting the animals at the farm and dressing up in pioneer clothes. You can chat with costumed interpreters or help the printmaker work the machine that prints old-fashioned scenes

KEEP IN MIND To experience the village as an 1860s family, book tickets months ahead for the popular Christmas by Lamplight evenings. Taste a sugarplum in a gaslit home, cheer on a performance in the Town Hall, or join the strolling Victorian carollers for a sing-along. It's a magical special event.

HEY, KIDS! Have you ever wanted to ask questions of a real farmer? Find out when the people who look after the farm animals are free to talk. They'll be able to tell you neat things such as "Seven Uses for a Goose." Can you guess? Let's see—eggs to eat, feathers for quill pens, comforters, and feather dusters, and of course, eating the goose at a special feast. You'll also be able to help feed the chickens, turkeys, and pigs. Now what does a guinea fowl or a Yorkshire pig eat?

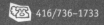 1000 Murray Ross Parkway

 $9 adults, $7 students, $5 children 5 and up

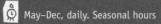 May–Dec, daily. Seasonal hours

 416/736–1733

 2 and up

on paper. Children can take them home to colour. On special days, the Games on the Green brings out the stilts, the hoops and sticks, and the quoits for old-fashioned croquet. A barn holds the action inside on rainy days.

Black Creek Pioneer Village also hosts a number of special events: Howling Hootenanny in October is the scene of pumpkin carving, a haunted maze, and ghost walks with ghostly tales about some of the 19th-century homes; Christmas Remembered from late November to the end of December when you'll be introduced to some uncommon holiday traditions like the kissing bough—oh, no!—and the popular Christmas by Lamplight. Many families return year after year with their own punched tin lamps that they purchased from the tinsmith at Black Creek.

EATS FOR KIDS If working on the farm engenders a hearty appetite, stop in at **The Half Way House Inn** (tel. 416/736–1733), which used to be the stomping grounds for stage-coach passengers travelling the King's Highway between Ontario and Quebec. Warm bread from the oven accompanies soups and stews. Beside the Inn is **The Bbq** serving hot dogs during the summer and on spring and fall weekends. There's an outdoor patio. The **Coffee Cart** sells snacks and sandwiches.

BLUFFER'S PARK

Do your kids long to feel the sand between their toes, walk along a windswept beach to collect driftwood, hike through paths strewn with cat-o-nine-tails taller than they are? Try Bluffer's Park, more a beach than a park, spread out beneath the 200-ft-high (61-m) Scarborough Cathedral Bluffs. This sculptured 15-km (9-mi) stretch of Lake Ontario shoreline offers grassy picnic areas, a marina, and duck ponds testing a new water filtration system for stormwater. But the manmade park is best known for its natural wilderness of sand and surf.

Scarborough's Cathedral Bluffs are a geological phenomenon. Carved out by glacial action during the Ice Age some 12,000 years ago, the cliffs have been sculpted by wind, rain, and wave action ever since. Looking up at the sandstone-coloured bluffs edged with greenery, you'd swear you were far away—some say they are Canada's answer to England's White Cliffs of Dover. It's dangerous to walk around up top (every few years, daredevils scaling or descending the Bluffs are scooped up by rescue teams). Your kids will be safer at the bottom playing in the

KEEP IN MIND A fun, and safe, place for kids to enjoy a top view from the Bluffs is the nearby **Guild Inn** (191 Guildwood Parkway, tel. 416/261–3331). It's south of Kingston Road, five minutes east of Brimley. Founded by Rosa and Spencer Clark as a haven for artists, the hotel has a garden filled with curious abandoned architectural pieces from torn–down buildings. Let the kids perform on the stage lined with Ionic columns from the old Bank of Toronto, or in summer, attend a children's play acted by a professional troupe. The gardens and high trails are spectacular.

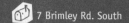 7 Brimley Rd. South

 Free, free parking

 Daily, sunrise–sunset, beach bathrooms open 9–9

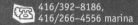 416/392-8186, 416/266-4556 marina

 All ages

waves, collecting snails along the shoreline, or watching for Monarch butterflies and migrating birds during the spring and fall (falls sees the butterflies gather en masse for a trip across the lake).

There is a supervised swimming area along the sand beach, bike and hiking paths past wildflowers and poplar trees, seagulls and fish galore, and lots of space for a soccer or a Frisbee game. Thanks to environmental groups and governments, native trees have been planted to attract wildlife such as rabbits and foxes; rocks and rubble in lakeside areas provide a hiding place for fish. Over 50 charter vessels stand by to take you out onto the lake to catch huge salmon. The sailing boats cutting the water are steered by students from the Performance Sailing School.

Even on a misty, foggy day, the park becomes a mysterious, dramatic setting that's ideal for ducks—and kids.

GETTING THERE Take Kingston Road east past Victoria Park Ave. to Brimley Road, turn south, and continue down the hill to the parking lots for Bluffer's Park. By transit, take the Kingston Road 12 bus from the Victoria Park subway station to the intersection of Brimley Road and Barkdene Hills, then walk south on Brimley to the park (a 10–15 minute walk downhill).

EATS FOR KIDS Many families bring picnics for the beach or eat at the tables set up on the grassy areas. A snack bar serving burgers, sausages, chicken fingers, and ice cream is open May–August 11–8:30. But for a great view of the marina and the bluffs, you can't do better than a windowside table or the patio at the lighthouselike **Bluffer's Restaurant** and **Dogfish Bar** (tel. 416/264-2337). It's the perfect setting for fish and chips, scallops, shrimp, the catch of the day, as well as kids' meals and Sunday brunch. It's open daily 11:30–3, 5–10 except January and February.

CASA LOMA

59

Sir Henry Pellatt's beloved, wacky but wonderful castle on the hill is a fitting testament to his rags-to-riches-and-back life. As the founder of the Toronto Electric Light Company in 1883 and chairman of 21 companies by 1901, the local financier could well afford to build his dream castle modeled after those he had seen in Europe. From 1910 to 1913, some 300 men (including craftsmen from Germany, stone masons from Scotland, and wood carvers from Italy) labored to construct one of the largest houses in North America on the highest point in Toronto. This monstrosity was the talk of the town.

The plans called for 98 rooms, 30 bathrooms, and 5,000 electric lights illuminating turrets and battlements and a stained-glass ceiling dome imported from Italy. Amusements included bowling alleys, a swimming pool, and a terrace that was frozen over in winter for skating and curling. The first privately owned electric elevator in Canada rose up just a few floors for Lady Pellatt's convenience, and one oven was big enough to cook an ox. With 59 telephones, the castle switchboard handled more calls than the city operator.

EATS FOR KIDS At **The Castle Café** (tel. 416/975–8388), pick up snacks and drinks for a picnic in the gardens or head to St. Clair and Yonge for fast food restaurants. For food as exotic as Casa Loma, try the curries, and homemade ice cream, at **Indian Rice Factory** (414 Dupont St., tel. 416/961–3472).

HEY, KIDS! Sir Henry really loved his horses. Can you see the herringbone pattern of tiles in the stables' floor? That's so the horses wouldn't slip. What about the windows over the stalls? They open upward to prevent drafts of wind. He even made 18-carat gold leaf nameplates for Indian Chief, Casa Loma Belle, Prince (his favourite), and the other horses. The stables are also special because during World War II, they were used as an assembly place for a secret sonar device used to detect German submarines. No one ever suspected. You might spot parts of the stables in the movie X-Men, one of many movies shot here.

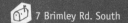 7 Brimley Rd. South

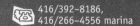 416/392–8186,
416/266–4556 marina

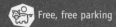 Free, free parking

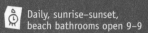 Daily, sunrise–sunset,
beach bathrooms open 9–9

 All ages

waves, collecting snails along the shoreline, or watching for Monarch butterflies and migrating birds during the spring and fall (falls sees the butterflies gather en masse for a trip across the lake).

There is a supervised swimming area along the sand beach, bike and hiking paths past wildflowers and poplar trees, seagulls and fish galore, and lots of space for a soccer or a Frisbee game. Thanks to environmental groups and governments, native trees have been planted to attract wildlife such as rabbits and foxes; rocks and rubble in lakeside areas provide a hiding place for fish. Over 50 charter vessels stand by to take you out onto the lake to catch huge salmon. The sailing boats cutting the water are steered by students from the Performance Sailing School.

Even on a misty, foggy day, the park becomes a mysterious, dramatic setting that's ideal for ducks—and kids.

GETTING THERE Take Kingston Road east past Victoria Park Ave. to Brimley Road, turn south, and continue down the hill to the parking lots for Bluffer's Park. By transit, take the Kingston Road 12 bus from the Victoria Park subway station to the intersection of Brimley Road and Barkdene Hills, then walk south on Brimley to the park (a 10–15 minute walk downhill).

EATS FOR KIDS Many families bring picnics for the beach or eat at the tables set up on the grassy areas. A snack bar serving burgers, sausages, chicken fingers, and ice cream is open May–August 11–8:30. But for a great view of the marina and the bluffs, you can't do better than a windowside table or the patio at the lighthouselike **Bluffer's Restaurant** and **Dogfish Bar** (tel. 416/264–2337). It's the perfect setting for fish and chips, scallops, shrimp, the catch of the day, as well as kids' meals and Sunday brunch. It's open daily 11:30–3, 5–10 except January and February.

CASA LOMA

Sir Henry Pellatt's beloved, wacky but wonderful castle on the hill is a fitting testament to his rags-to-riches-and-back life. As the founder of the Toronto Electric Light Company in 1883 and chairman of 21 companies by 1901, the local financier could well afford to build his dream castle modeled after those he had seen in Europe. From 1910 to 1913, some 300 men (including craftsmen from Germany, stone masons from Scotland, and wood carvers from Italy) labored to construct one of the largest houses in North America on the highest point in Toronto. This monstrosity was the talk of the town.

The plans called for 98 rooms, 30 bathrooms, and 5,000 electric lights illuminating turrets and battlements and a stained-glass ceiling dome imported from Italy. Amusements included bowling alleys, a swimming pool, and a terrace that was frozen over in winter for skating and curling. The first privately owned electric elevator in Canada rose up just a few floors for Lady Pellatt's convenience, and one oven was big enough to cook an ox. With 59 telephones, the castle switchboard handled more calls than the city operator.

EATS FOR KIDS At **The Castle Café** (tel. 416/975–8388), pick up snacks and drinks for a picnic in the gardens or head to St. Clair and Yonge for fast food restaurants. For food as exotic as Casa Loma, try the curries, and homemade ice cream, at **Indian Rice Factory** (414 Dupont St., tel. 416/961–3472).

HEY, KIDS! Sir Henry really loved his horses. Can you see the herringbone pattern of tiles in the stables' floor? That's so the horses wouldn't slip. What about the windows over the stalls? They open upward to prevent drafts of wind. He even made 18-carat gold leaf nameplates for Indian Chief, Casa Loma Belle, Prince (his favourite), and the other horses. The stables are also special because during World War II, they were used as an assembly place for a secret sonar device used to detect German submarines. No one ever suspected. You might spot parts of the stables in the movie X-Men, one of many movies shot here.

 1 Austin Terrace

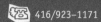 416/923–1171

 $10 adults, $6.50 youth 14–17, $6 children 4–13

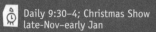 Daily 9:30–4; Christmas Show late-Nov–early Jan

 3 and up

Kids have free reign of the secret passageways behind mahogany panels, a 240-m-long (800-ft-long) underground tunnel to the stables, and staircases up to the turrets with 39.5-m-high (130-ft-high) views. Sir Henry collected suits of armour and several are scattered about along with military medals and antiques such as a copy of the Coronation Throne in Westminster Abbey. The gardens are also impressive. Here, kids can search for the secret garden as well as squirrels, birds, and even garter snakes.

Alas, Sir Henry's folly turned out to be folly. He had intended to spend $250,000. But the final result ate up $3.5 million of Sir Henry's money—equivalent to about $44 million today—and the house in which he lived for 10 years was far from finished. When he died in 1939 at the age of 80, he was living in a room in Mimico (a Toronto suburb) with not a lot of money in the bank. The Kiwanis Club of Casa Loma has maintained the castle since 1937.

KEEP IN MIND Your kids may enjoy the self-guided audio tour. It's included in the admission price. Younger children will be wide-eyed at holiday time when performers, magicians, clowns, and Santa romp in a fairy tale setting. Strollers are not recommended due to all the stairs. For a memorable keepsake, look in the gift shop for *The White Stone in the Castle Wall* by author Sheldon Oberman. This beautifully illustrated children's book provides an artistic interpretation as to why Sir Henry allowed one white stone to be placed among the 249,999 others in the wall surrounding the castle.

CBC BEHIND-THE-SCENES TOUR

I f you're watching TV or listening to radio in Toronto, you're sure to flick across the Canadian Broadcasting Corporation, or, as it's affectionately known, the CBC. With two television networks (English and French), two radio stations, two 24-hour news channels, and a northern service, this corporation is Canada's largest cultural institution. At the English network headquarter's digs in downtown Toronto (the French headquarters is in Montreal), you can now take a tour of one of the first fully digital broadcasting centres in the world.

The tour starts with a 150-ft elevator ride up to the high-tech studios where news, comedy shows, and kids' shows are filmed. Although junior TV viewers may not be so impressed with the statistics—four football fields of floor on each level, 3,000 Neoprene rubber vibration pads which support the building, enough cable to stretch all the way from Toronto to Edmonton—their attention is won over by the live newsroom, the coffee shop set for the *Royal Canadian Air Farce* with its real doughnuts, and the huge freight elevator that once delivered a horse to a stage set.

KEEP IN MIND Don't leave without showing the kids some of your television and radio roots at the excellent CBC Museum on the ground floor (416/205–5574; open M–F 9–5, Sa 12–4). Admission is free. Rotating exhibits might allow kids to put on a puppet show in a 1950s TV studio, announce a radio show on an authentic 1940 microphone, or listen to a nonsense song from a time when families gathered round the radio. A wall of TVs replays famous historical moments—JFK's assassination in 1963, Terry Fox's run across Canada in 1980, or Nelson Mandela being freed from prison in 1990.

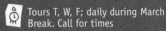

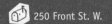 250 Front St. W.

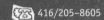 416/205–8605

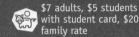 $7 adults, $5 students with student card, $20 family rate

 Tours T, W, F; daily during March Break. Call for times

7 and up

Although it's never guaranteed, you could bump into some familiar faces as you enter the lobby and stroll through the soaring 10-story Atrium. Part of the fun is not knowing what or whom you'll come across. You might see a "live" Olympic table tennis trial, young actors from the *Our Hero* television show, or Irish rock superstars guesting on a radio show. Because the ground floor also serves as a live TV studio and a local radio recording studio, broadcasters and newsmakers are constantly coming and going. The list of the famous who have at one time worked at CBC is legendary—comedian Mike Myers, funny man Jim Carrey, actor Lorne Greene of *Ponderosa* fame, *Dudley Doo-Right's* Leslie Nielsen, and *Saturday Night Live* alumna Gilda Radner to name a few.

The tour lasts about an hour, not enough time to answer every technical question, but enough to get a glimpse of what goes on behind the screen.

HEY, KIDS! Want some help with your homework? Check out the CBC's Web site just for kids 8–14 at www.cbc4kids.ca. As well as stories, quizzes, and games such as Guess the Instrument, the What's New section offers homework tips and info.

EATS FOR KIDS Grab a bite where some of the journalists do at the **Ooh La La Café** (tel. 416/979–7122) on the ground floor of the Atrium. The made-to-order sandwiches or hot dishes can be eaten outside in summer. Two small kids could picnic on the quirky statue-sculpture bench outside with bronzed Glenn Gould, the famous pianist, ready to share a sandwich. Across the street is **Planet Hollywood** (277 Front St. W., tel. 416/596–7827) for more celebrity swish. *See also* Air Canada Centre, CN Tower, and SkyDome for restaurants within walking distance.

CN TOWER

57

You just can't get away from the CN Tower, the world's tallest free-standing structure that was named one of the "Seven Wonders of the Modern World" in a survey of civil engineers. From the air, the water, and miles north of the city, you can see its needle nose rising up to a colossal 553 m (1,815 ft). Before too long, your kids will be asking to climb onboard one of the six glass-fronted elevators and rocket up to the Look Out, 346 m (1,136 ft) above the city, in 58 seconds flat. The view is worth it. You'll spy Matchbox-like cars roving the city streets, rooftop gardens, tiny baseball players in the SkyDome, and boats sailing around the harbour like toys in a bathtub.

One floor below is the biggest hit with kids, the Glass Floor with its observation deck. Tiptoe out onto the 23.8 sq m (256 sq ft) of solid glass to look straight down to terra firma. You'll be reassured to know that the floor could withstand the weight of 14 large hippos, though how they tested that is a mystery. From the Sky Pod ($7.14 extra),

HEY, KIDS! Race you up the top? The CN Tower has the world's longest metal staircase. Once or twice a year, people walk up the 1,776 steps, especially to raise money for charity. How long would it take? Brendan Keenoy did it in only 7 minutes, 52 seconds to set the world record!

EATS FOR KIDS If your stomach can handle it after the exciting elevator rides, you have a host of options: **Horizons Café** on the Look Out Level offers "Towering Thirst Quenchers," kid-friendly wraps, pasta, chicken fingers, and pie in the sky for dessert; **360 Restaurant** (tel. 416/362–5411), the highest revolving restaurant on the planet, offers scrumptious fare and an unmatched view, especially at sunset. If you're on a budget, pick up multicultural fast food such as *panini* sandwiches, flatbread filled with vegetables, and cafeteria pizza fare at the ground-level **Marketplace Café**.

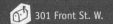

301 Front St. W.

$15.99 ages 13 and up,
$10.99 ages 4–12; rides
$7.50 ages 4 and up

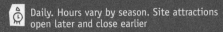

Daily. Hours vary by season. Site attractions
open later and close earlier

416/868–6937

3 and up

another 33 storeys up, a clear day lets you see 120 km (75 mi) away to the mist rising
from Niagara Falls. On the way down, the elevator travels at the same speed as a military
parachute descending to earth.

You don't have to go up the Tower for the kids to have a good time. You can journey
across Canada via a 20-minute film or watch a movie about the tower's construction in
the Maple Leaf Cinema ($7.50). Two new motion simulator rides have joined the
simulated game experiences in The Themed Arcade. Do you want to be an Indy racer,
Olympic downhill skier or snowboarder, or dinosaur chaser? The Marketplace gift shop
is one of the best in the city. Memorable souvenirs range from good quality T-shirts
to books about Native peoples to the ultimate Canadian memento—maple syrup in
a sky-high glass CN Tower bottle.

KEEP IN MIND Because this is Toronto's top tourist attraction
with two million visitors each year, arrive early or in the off-season to avoid
lineups for the elevators. There are some super photo ops here so don't forget the camera. How about your kids standing in front of a picture of the CN
Tower being bombarded with lightning bolts (lightning safely strikes the tower
up to 65 times each year) or striking a lie-down pose on the glass floor with
the city some 342 m (1,122 ft) below?

CENTREVILLE AMUSEMENT PARK

This small amusement park on Centre Island is perfect for children not ready to loop the loop or do the drop at Paramount Canada's Wonderland. Built around a re-created turn-of-the-20th-century town, Centreville has everything a small town fair should—balloons, candy cotton, agricultural exhibits, a boat ride, and an antique carousel. Your preteens might barely tolerate the scene and head for the bumper cars, the mini-golf, and the log flume descent down a water slide. But your little ones will love it.

A popular activity is lazily steering a Swan Boat around a lagoon that's dripping with weeping willow trees. Another hit is the miniature train. Your legs will be scrunched as the train toots and clangs and screeches its way through intersections, over a duck pond, and through a dark tunnel. But the experience is worth it. And don't miss the Antique Carousel made in Germantown, Pennsylvania in 1908; it's one of only 30 in the world. Let your child choose between a hand-carved prancing rabbit, a pink pig, a grey pussycat, or a traditional jumping horse that whirls to Wurlitzer organ music.

HEY, KIDS! At old-fashioned fairs, judges used to give prizes to the animals. Remember *Charlotte's Web?* Centreville has animals, too, like Wilbur the pig at its Far Enough Farm. It looks just like a real farm with a red barn, an old tractor, and roosters that crow even in the afternoon. Look for the new babies born every year. You might see baby piglets, baby bunnies, baby goats called kids, or baby calfs. Some are tame, like the donkeys. But some, like the police horses, do bite. So ask before you reach out to award your animal a friendly pat.

Centre Island

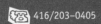 416/203-0405

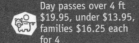 Day passes over 4 ft
$19.95, under $13.95,
families $16.25 each
for 4

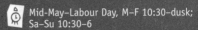 Mid-May–Labour Day, M–F 10:30–dusk;
Sa–Su 10:30–6

up to 10

The best thing about Centreville is that this park is small—about 20 rides—and a family outing won't necessarily break the bank. Instead of shelling out for an all-day pass, you can buy individual tickets at 60 cents each (50 tickets for $28), a good option for a toddler who's not quite sure about amusement park rides. The attractions cost between two and six tickets, from the Little Dipper Boat ride to the Lake Monster Coaster (restricted to those over 4 ft). Two of the best are free—the large wading pool surrounded by grass, and Far Enough Farm at the eastern end of the park. Here, roosters crow and strut, baby goats tussle, piglets grunt and snuggle into the mud. Centreville offers simple entertainment but to a young child, it's more fun than the biggest rollercoaster on the planet.

KEEP IN MIND
The Island ferries carry up to 1,000 passengers and they are jam-packed on weekends and holidays. If you want a relaxed, uncrowded visit with space to spare, aim to set out early or, even better, on a weekday.

EATS FOR KIDS Two on-site restaurants, the **Island Paradise** by the ferry docks (tel. 416/203-0245) and the **Iroquois Grill** near Centreville (tel. 416/203-8795) have children's menus and scenic views from their outdoor tables, but it's probably quicker and cheaper to take advantage of the food booths in the amusement park—Italian sausage, pizza, funnel cakes, tortilla wraps, and ice cream—or picnic under the trees by the swan boats. You could also barbecue hot dogs or burgers if you want to carry over charcoal brickets and a cooler. To reserve a grill, call tel. 416/392-8188.

CHILDREN'S OWN MUSEUM

If kids had a wish list for their perfect play space, the Children's Own Museum (COM) would meet every request. There's a pint-size town with a supermarket and a veterinary hospital with real X-rays, a tree house in which to hide away, an art room filled with paints, a theatre with umpteen costume changes available, and finally, a room filled with books for snuggling-up story times. Everything is kid–size from the tiny tables and chairs to the paint brushes.

It's no accident that there are no interactive exhibits, no buttons to push, no computer games or gizmos. Instead, more old-fashioned kinds of fun rule the day. Founded by early childhood education specialist Geraldine Mabin and committed parents, the museum fosters learning through play and encourages social interactions. It's a chance for all the senses to work at once and the children love it. Just sit back and laugh as your kids revel in goop, slime, and dough during Ooey Gooey Messy Fun experiments.

KEEP IN MIND The museum is busy during holiday times, so you may run into lines and timed tickets. If you have to pull your kids away from this place, consider a Children's Own Museum annual family membership. The $85 fee includes unlimited admission for a family of five, newsletter mailings, and discounts in the gift shop.

EATS FOR KIDS With Bloor St. right at the doorstep, there are several choices for this age group. Try family-friendly **Mövenpick** (133 Yorkville Ave., tel. 416/926–9545) one block north for fun animal mask menus and good food. **Lox, Stock & Bagel** in the Hazelton Lanes shopping complex (55 Avenue Rd., tel. 416/968–8850) serves—you guessed it—upscale bagels. For dessert, there's no debate. Ice-cream fans agree that **Greg's Ice Cream** (200 Bloor St. W., tel. 416/961–4734) scoops up some of the city's best. His inventive flavours include mango, banana chocolate chunk, and roasted marshmallow.

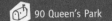90 Queen's Park

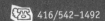416/542-1492

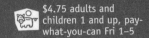$4.75 adults and children 1 and up, pay-what-you-can Fri 1–5

Daily 10–5

2–8

You'll also find some of the most inventive programming in town. Neighbourhood professionals like bakers and doctors drop in to give talks and presentations. The Fall Festival offers barn dancing in the outside Plaza with an old-time square dance caller. Sing Along Sundays feature songs, finger plays, and poetry set to music. Most special activities are free. Some, such as woodworking workshops, charge a small fee.

The Children's Own Museum is also working at becoming a resource for parents. While Junior curls up with *The Very Hungry Caterpillar*, you can consult the latest parent manual. Parents' workshops cover ideas, advice, and discussions on the value of play or "Why Art"? It's nice just to hang out here. Your kids will have a whale of a time and you'll pick up a few tips on how to encourage that sort of satisfying simple play.

HEY, KIDS! Did you like doing something special or seeing something unusual or meeting someone interesting at the museum? You can tell the directors what you liked. Some kids reported that they liked acting the bride on the stage or loved building in the building site. Others said they liked the big tree. Since this is a children's museum, kids are important here. Even little kids can offer ideas and suggestions, and make things for the museum such as the crawly junkyard bugs for the new outdoor garden.

CHINATOWN

Digging a hole won't get you to China, but a walk along Spadina Avenue in Chinatown brings you pretty close. You may as well be in another world: street signs are in Chinese characters, sculptures of dragons and Asian lions guard doorways, and the noisy chattering of a foreign language and the smells of unknown foods allow even native Torontonians to feel as if they've left their city. Toronto is home to North America's largest Chinese population and though only a third of the city's half million Asians live along these streets, many come from outlying areas to do their shopping and conduct their business here.

For a child, it's a unique if overwhelming experience, especially when the sidewalks are crowded and the rapid-fire negotiations over price and quality are at their peak. The best way to explore is by foot, with your hand wrapped tightly around those of your smaller children so they won't suddenly be swept along with the crowd. Start your journey at the corner of Spadina Avenue and Dundas Street, then radiate along both sides of

KEEP IN MIND If your kids like Chinatown, they may want to explore other interesting Toronto neighbourhoods. Greek Town, along Danforth Avenue between Chester and Pape, is alive on warm evenings when Greek families come out to saunter along the sidewalks. Most of the restaurants offer outdoor patios. Little India on eastern Gerrard is an interesting shopping strip where kids can buy jewelled bangles or Indian CDs. Little Italy along College Street West is known for its eateries and ice-cream parlours like the Sicilian Ice Cream Company (712 College St. W., tel. 416/531-7716).

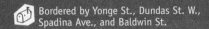 Bordered by Yonge St., Dundas St. W., Spadina Ave., and Baldwin St.

 Free

 Daily

 No phone

 All ages

each of these streets. You'll find baskets of strange-looking vegetables and fruits, brown glazed ducks hanging in restaurant windows, boxes of dried fish, and mountains of spices. At curio shops, a little bit of money will garner an embroidered silk purse, a stick of incense, a pair of chopsticks, a painted fan, or a puzzle toy.

As you walk along, you'll see lots of red for good luck and octagonal-shape mirrors on homes or storefronts to ward off evil spirits. For more good fortune, stop at one of the bakeries along Dundas like Kim Moon (438 Dundas St. W., tel. 416/977–1933) or Tung Hing Bakery (428 Dundas St. W., tel. 416/593–9375) for a moon cake. Enjoyed during August or September when the moon is at its brightest, these sweet or savoury filled cakes symbolize good luck.

HEY, KIDS! Chinese kids celebrate New Year's twice—once on January 1 and again according to the Chinese calendar, sometime between Jan 21 and Feb 20. Each year is ruled by a different animal sign like a dragon or a rabbit. People say that babies born during that year have personalities similar to the ruling animal. Under which animal do you think you were born?

EATS FOR KIDS There are so many Chinese and Vietnamese restaurants along these streets that it's hard to choose. All welcome children. For inexpensive family fare, try **Happy Seven** (358 Spadina Ave., tel. 416/971–9820). For an all-out feast of Peking duck, one of the best is **The Champion House Restauraunt** (480 Dundas St. W., tel. 416/977–8282). The kids will love the ceremonial ringing of the gong as each duck emerges from the kitchen. For Dim Sum, little bites from bamboo steamers, stop at **Chinese Palace Restaurant** (150 Dundas St. W., tel. 416/977–3750).

CITY CENTRE AIRPORT

The Toronto City Centre Airport is straight out of the *Casablanca* film set. You almost expect Humphrey Bogart to emerge from one of the prop planes. At one time, this downtown airstrip on Hanlan's Point was slated to become the city's major airport. Today, it looks laughingly small. But it's big enough to launch 41 Air Ontario commercial passenger flights each week to Ottawa, Montreal, and London as well as handle hundreds of takeoffs and landings each day by the small planes parked along the airstrip.

For a young airplane fanatic, this place is heaven. Even when crossing over on the Maple City ferry, they'll be able to see planes circling in the sky. Head for the terminal building to sit in front of Druxy's window with a drink. Lined up along the airstrip, the tiny planes look like Matchbox toys. On the outdoor patio, it can be windy and noisy as the propellors rev up; you'll definitely catch a whiff of fuel. You might also see the

EATS FOR KIDS The only place to eat at the airport is **Druxy's** (tel. 416/703–1032) on the second floor of the terminal building. It's known for its deli sandwiches. Soup, pastas, and homemade cookies complement the pastrami on rye. It closes at 4PM on Saturday, and at 5PM on Sunday.

KEEP IN MIND This outing is best on weekday afternoons when the airport is busiest and there's lots of flying action. Sundays are very quiet. If you really want to give your kids a thrill, book a Heli-Tours ride in a helicopter that takes off and lands right at the City Centre Airport. A six- to eight-minute ride on the whirlybird over the Toronto islands costs from $54 and up. You can take all kinds of tours from The Helicopter Company (tel. 416/203–3280) such as their Heli-Picnic Tour with lunch at the Kortright Centre, or Vertical Obsession, a 12-minute ride over the skyscrapers of downtown.

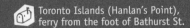 Toronto Islands (Hanlan's Point), ferry from the foot of Bathurst St.

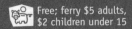 Free; ferry $5 adults, $2 children under 15

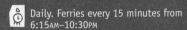 Daily. Ferries every 15 minutes from 6:15AM–10:30PM

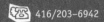 416/203–6942

 4–9

ambulance helicopter, planes from the flying school, the police copters, sightseeing tour flights, and seaplanes. There's action around the water too as the ducks or seagulls swim about. "Is it a bird, or is it a plane?" At the City Centre Airport it could be both.

The original 1939 terminal building is a National Historic Site that attracts aviation buffs from around the world. It served as a training base for the Royal Norwegian Air Force during World War II. Over 2,657 fliers practised here before returning to Europe to fight. But aside from reading the historic plaques, you won't need much time for touring. The fun here for kids is in watching the pilots come and go, seeing the Dash-8's turbo-props taxi down the runways, or the million-dollar helicopters start their engines and take off into the sky.

HEY, KIDS! Did you know that the ferry crossing to the island airport is listed in the *Guinness Book of World Records* as the world's shortest scheduled ferry ride? It takes only 2 minutes to make it across the water. And that's when it's rough. When it's calm, the ferry can make the 122 m (400 ft) distance in under 30 seconds. The city leaders keep talking about building a tunnel or a bridge to the airport. But the ferry is more fun, don't you think?

CRAWFORD LAKE CONSERVATION AREA & IROQUOIAN VILLAGE

Walking into the impressive Turtle Clan Longhouse, as tall as it is long, it's the smells that take hold—the pungent mingling of fur, a smoky fire, dried corn and herbs, cedar boughs laid on sleeping berths, and an earthern floor. Definitely not the smells of the modern home. As the smoke clears and your eyes adjust, you'll see a large interior where perhaps 35 or 40 women, men, and children lived together. It's authentically re-created (save for the uncluttered floor) and your kids will think they've stepped into another world. And they have.

The Iroquois Village, dating from between 1434 and 1459, was discovered almost by accident in the 1970s when researchers were investigating the nearby unusual lake (given its wonderful shimmering colour due to limited oxygen at the bottom). Upon finding an inordinate amount of corn pollen in the lake's sediments, archaeologists surmised that Native peoples must have settled here and started digging. Today, you can see some of the artifacts, visit the two longhouses, watch videos, and try to imagine what life was

KEEP IN MIND Nearby is Mountsberg Conservation Area (tel. 905/854–2276) with wagon rides, demonstrations of birds of prey, 14 km (9 mi) of hiking trails, farm animals, and family activities. During Maple Season, you can experience both the Iroquois and Pioneer traditions in one day.

 Steeles Ave. and
Guelph Line

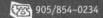 905/854-0234

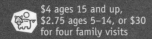 $4 ages 15 and up,
$2.75 ages 5–14, or $30
for four family visits

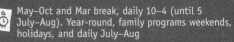 May–Oct and Mar break, daily 10–4 (until 5
July–Aug). Year-round, family programs weekends,
holidays, and daily July–Aug

 3 and up

like when families shared space, food, heat, and even pets.

Like the First Nation peoples' lives, the Conservation Area's special programs revolve around the seasons. Every weekend and daily in summer, children can try the seasonal Discovery Challenge (a visual scavenger hunt with prizes), as well as craft making, storytelling sessions, or nature activities. Learn how maple syrup was boiled in Sweet Water Season (March); take a wildflower walk in the Season of Many Frogs Peeping (May); hear Iroquoian legends; play the uproarious native game of Snow Snakes (a miniature bobsled game down an icy track) or snowshoe along the trails in winter. (Snowshoes are available for adults or kids eight and up.) As you walk the Bruce Trail, or stroll around the lake on the wooden boardwalk, you'll probably agree that this spiritual setting was a great place to call home.

GETTING THERE Take Highway 401 west to Guelph Line Exit 312. Turn south to Steeles Avenue and travel east to the Conservation Area entrance.

HEY, KIDS! Do you know who the Three Sisters are? They are corn, pole beans, and squash, always planted together and harvested each fall. If the Iroquoian people planted good amounts of these three vegetables, families could always survive the harsh winters with enough food.

CULLEN GARDENS & MINIATURE VILLAGE

How many times in their young lives do kids get to feel like giants? Among some 160 miniature buildings all peopled with teeny, tiny citizens, kids tower over the train stations and town halls, the amusement parks and cottages. Though adults tag along to this attraction for its dazzling displays of daffodils, tulips, chrysanthemums, and topiaries, children are enchanted with the dollhouse-size re-creation of a typical Southern Ontario town. It's the most popular tourist attraction between Toronto Zoo and Kingston, Ontario, and every year it just keeps on getting bigger.

Look for the realistic highlights: the firemen squirting water from a tiny hose to put out a flickering fire, the amusement park with its Ferris wheel and flying swings, a water-skier in cottage country being pulled by a Lilliputian motorboat. There's even a parade

GETTING THERE Take Highway 401 east to Brock Street (Exit 410), turn north to Taunton Road (Highway 4), then turn west to the village.

HEY, KIDS! The craftspeople use all kinds of tricks to make these miniature people and homes. Did you know that the hundreds of tiny persons start out as wire curtain hooks that are bent into shape? Then epoxy putty is added and molded to make faces, arms, and legs. A flickering electric light makes the imitation fire, and a kerosene-dipped mosquito coil creates the smoke. Some things are real though, like the tiny shingles on the roofs, the plants around the houses, and the tiny TV tuned to a real channel in the television shop on Main Street.

 300 Taunton Rd. W.

 905/686-1600

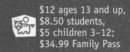 $12 ages 13 and up,
$8.50 students,
$5 children 3–12;
$34.99 Family Pass

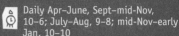 Daily Apr–June, Sept–mid-Nov,
10–6; July–Aug, 9–8; mid-Nov–early
Jan, 10–10

 1–13

down Main Street with a marching band. Follow the trains that whistle by under bridges and along the tracks. In wintertime, the tiny figures don winter coats to throw snowballs and line up for the Santa Claus Parade. If you feel like singing "It's a Small World After All," go ahead. The whole village is built on a 1:12 scale.

There's lots to do here besides playing Big Friendly Giant, so plan a lengthy visit if you want to take a tractor-pulled pioneer wagon ride, explore the bike and trike trails, play mini-golf, catch frogs in the pond along the wildflower walk, and get soaked in the Splash and Sprinkler pools. Most weekends and holidays, you'll find activities related to the season such as the pumpkin carving and corn roasts in the fall, or fireworks in the summer, not miniature in the least.

KEEP IN MIND Cullen Gardens becomes a fairyland of lights from mid-November to early January. It's a magical time to visit. More than 100,000 strands of lights decorate the village while motion light displays imitate a sleigh riding through the woods, an owl flying, or a miniature train that puffs smoke. Of course, you'll find Santa and Mrs. Claus in residence, and outside down the hill, a Nativity scene with live animals. Friday night is Kids Night with face painting and entertainment.

DAVID DUNLAP OBSERVATORY

The David Dunlap Observatory houses Canada's largest optical telescope. When it was first opened in 1935, it was the largest in the world. Donated by Mrs. Jessie Dunlap in honour of her late husband who was a lawyer and amateur astonomer, the observatory has Friday night star-gazing evenings especially for families, as well as Saturday night tours.

It's best to visit on a night when the sky is clear. On cloudy nights, participants can learn about the telescope but will not be able to look through the eyepiece. If it's a nice evening, there's another bonus. Members of the Royal Astronomical Society often come out on clear nights to set up their equipment on the front lawn of the Observatory. When you look at the selected portion of sky through the large, 23-tonne telescope, the heavens may look cloudy rather than punctuated by points of light. But if you view the same celestial objects through a small telescope with a large field of view, it's clearer and more impressive. However, your children will be impressed just to be in contact with the gigantic telescope. Its whirrings and turnings open a giant eye to the sky.

HEY, KIDS! When the observatory opened in 1935, it amazed people. The whole dome could rotate 360 degrees in eight minutes (it still does). It also had the world's largest telescope; its concave mirror alone weighs two tonnes, about the same weight as an elephant. The reflector telescope works like this: A large concave mirror collects and concentrates light. A second mirror reflects the light to the eye lens. Today, the Herschel telescope in the Canary Islands off the coast of Africa uses electronic cameras and computers to see stars in the sky. No matter how big or strong the telescope we use, light from the stars still has to travel for thousands of years before reaching our eyes.

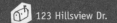 123 Hillsview Dr.

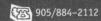 905/884-2112

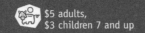 $5 adults,
$3 children 7 and up

 Early June–late Sept, F and Sa at dusk.
Call for exact times

 10 and up

Although the family tours are recommended for kids over seven, the lecture that starts off the evening, given by graduate astronomy students from the University of Toronto, may be somewhat dry and scientific for kids under 10. If you have a star and galaxy nut, he or she will be fine. Children are encouraged to throw out questions and they ask good ones: Do all stars die? What is the name of the biggest star? Can stars recycle their gases?

After the half-hour talk, it's off through the dark to the main dome, where everyone gets a turn to climb the stairs to the eyepiece. Your kids may not see the cow jumping over the moon, but it could begin a hobby that's as easy as going out the door and looking up at the sky.

GETTING THERE Take the Don Valley Parkway north to the 16th Avenue exit. Drive west to Bayview, then north to Hillsview Drive. Follow the signs to the Observatory.

KEEP IN MIND From October to April, tours are given on Thursday mornings for school groups from 10 to 11:30. You can often join in with a class if you make reservations in advance. You won't be able to look through the eyepiece but you will see the telescope.

DOUBLE-DECKER BUS TOURS

What better way to see the city sights than from the top of a double-decker bus? "Big hat, big hair?" asks the tour guide as the bus heads toward an overpass. "Duck," he shouts as the bus drives underneath, just missing heads by what seems like inches but is more like feet. Toronto's fleet of nine buses, run by Toronto Olde Towne Tours, offers a totally new perspective of the city. Riding high, kids can really get a closer look at the CN Tower, skyscrapers, or the St. James Cathedral balancing the second-highest church steeple in North America. Still, it's probably more fun looking down at pedestrians or at the public art decorating the sidewalks. Note the bronze hockey players in front of the Hockey Hall of Fame ready to jump over the boards.

A ticket allows hop-on hop-off privileges at 23 stops. You can buy your tickets at Stop #1, Nicholby's Welcome Centre (123 Front St. W.) or at any of the stops along the way. Your ticket is good for 24 hours so you can plan a two-day itinerary of family-friendly

KEEP IN MIND Riding up top is fun but be on guard when you're driving along under live overhead streetcar wires. If your children must reach out and touch everything, you might consider the hop-on hop-off Classic Turn of the Century Trolley ride instead, but it isn't as much fun.

EATS FOR KIDS There are lots of opportunities to jump off the bus for great family food breaks. The world's original **Hard Rock Cafe** is at stop 5 (283 Yonge St., tel. 416/362–3636), but more interesting might be the branch at the SkyDome, stop 23, overlooking the playing field (Gate 1, tel. 416/341–2388). Or, hop off at stop 4 for **Mr. Greenjeans** (the Eaton Centre, tel. 416/979–1212) or the **Pickle Barrel** (312 Yonge St., tel. 416/977–6677) for fun menus and large portions. *See* Chinatown or Hockey Hall of Fame for other good possibilities.

 123 Front St. W.

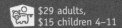 $29 adults,
$15 children 4–11

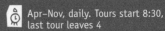 Apr–Nov, daily. Tours start 8:30, last tour leaves 4

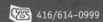 416/614-0999

 3 and up

attractions. No parking worries, or fighting traffic jams. Along the way, the guides tell jokes, entertain with anecdotes, and offer lots of information. Kids may be unimpressed with the historical lore, but they will delight in finding the grimacing gargoyle-like faces of the politicians carved into Old City Hall, or guessing if Toronto's weather beacon on the Canada Life building is forecasting foul or fair.

The most popular stop-off points for families are Casa Loma, the CN Tower, and the Yorkville shopping district where kids can shop for souvenirs at The Toy Shop, Kidding Awound, or Ice, a celebrity favourite for novelties (all on Cumberland). You'll also be able to hop off at the ROM, Bata Shoe Museum, Nathan Phillips Square, Historic Fort York, The Pier, Toronto's Waterfront Museum, and the SkyDome/Air Canada Centre. All of these top family destinations are profiled in this book. Then, just as you would in Jolly Old London, at your final stop, treat yourselves to a lolly or a nice cup of tea.

HEY, KIDS! If you pay attention to the tour guides, you will learn a lot. Why are some street signs blue and some yellow? Because the yellow ones follow the sun east to west and the blue ones run north and south to the lake. What was invented at Mt. Sinai Hospital? Pablum, the first cereal for babies. These are the kinds of interesting facts the guides know. After the tour, maybe your family can make up its own trivia game with pennies for prizes.

FANTASY FAIR

What to do with three kids under six on a blustery day? Planes and trains and automobiles—you'll find them all in miniature at Ontario's largest indoor amusement park. With an antique carousel, a bell-ringing train, bumper boats, the country's highest indoor Ferris wheel, and a giant play structure with slides, climbing nets, and the province's biggest ball pits, this shopping mall fair will satisfy both the timid and the brave.

Youngsters are thrilled to steer around a track in a fire engine, or be pushed around a small pool in mini–bumper boats by an attendant wearing hip waders. On the railroad circuit, little ones coast through a tunnel and wave to parents standing behind the real flashing signal lights and crossing guards. The Play Village has a Small Ball Crawl for kids three and under. There's not much here for those used to scream-inducing thrill rides. But for kids who have never been to an amusement park, or your preschoolers who want to ride by themselves, this contained park is perfect. Holidays bring special entertainments such as the Halloween Ride and Treat days, costume contests and December school holiday magic and puppet shows.

HEY, KIDS! The antique carousel has beautiful riding horses with jewelled eyes, but some carousels have other animals like rabbits and ostriches. Rabbits and ostriches, you ask? Well, you know you can't ride a rabbit. But you can ride an ostrich. In South Africa, people ride them in races. The riders wear special jockey outfits and hang on to the ostrich wings. On this carousel, it's easy to stay on the horse. Just grip with your knees, as you would with a real jumping horse, and hang on to the pole. After the ride is over, give your horse a friendly pat as thanks for a good ride.

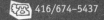

Every weekend, between 11 and 7, kids can turn into wizards or clowns with face painting.

Fantasy Fair is constructed as a Victorian village with a real ice-cream parlour, magnificent men in their flying machines overhead, and storefronts opening onto the streets. The turn-of-the-20th-century Looff Carousel is one of 40 carousels Charles Looff made between 1876 and 1916. This carousel was discovered in a storage room in California and is one of 13 remaining.

On a sunny day, light pours in through the skylights and floor-to-ceiling windows. It's reminiscent of being outside at a village fair. If the weather outdoors is truly awful, extend your visit with games in the Fantasy Station Arcade, shopping at the 180 stores and services in the mall, and catching a family movie at the Cineplex theatre complex.

GETTING THERE Woodbine is just across from Woodbine Race-track. Take the Gardiner Expressway (QEW) westbound to Highway 427 north. Continue to Rexdale Boulevard cutoff, then drive east to the Woodbine Centre parking lot. The entrance to Fantasy Fair is on the east side of the shopping centre.

KEEP IN MIND Try to come early or on weekdays to avoid the crowds. For instance, on a Tuesday afternoon, your railroader can ride the clanging train around the track as often as he likes. When it's busy, kids with an All-Day Pass may be restricted to one hour's play in the Play Village. At the Customer Care Centre, you can check coats and parcels or rent strollers at no extra charge. All you need is identification or a credit card. Next door is a nursing chair and change table and upstairs, birthday party rooms with play equipment and tables.

#506 STREETCAR RIDE

Ever since tracks were laid down to allow the city's horse-drawn streetcars a smoother ride, Torontonians have loved this way of travelling around the city. The first electric streetcar was invented in Toronto by John Wright, who showed it off at the 1883 Canadian National Exhibition. Although certain religious zealots once declared the Sunday streetcar to be the devil's chariot, there's no better way to spend a leisurely Saturday or Sunday than rumbling along some of the 313 km (194 mi) of track.

The city's busiest streetcar route, #506 from Main Station in the east end to High Park in the west, is a perfect route for sightseeing. You and the kids can travel the world from the Little India along Gerrard Street to Cabbagetown on Carlton Street, from Little Italy and Portuguese merchants along College Street to the Polish section along Roncesvalles Avenue, and finally, to High Park. Check out the jewelled bangles and shimmering saris hanging in the Little India shops, and the sidewalks spilling with

HEY, KIDS!

Here's some trivia: What did the first horsecar ride cost? 5 cents. What's the longest route? #501 Queen, 24.8 km (15.4 mi) from the Beaches to the Humber Loop on Queen Street West. How many people ride the streetcars each year? 80 million. That's almost three times the population of Canada.

EATS FOR KIDS
Feeling hungry? There are dozens of places to stop off along the way. If your youngsters are adventurous eaters, try the **Bar-Be-Que Hut** in Little India (1455 Gerrard St. E., tel. 416/466–0411) or the **Café Diplomatico** on College Street at Clinton (594 College St., tel. 416/534–4637). Along the way, there is a **McDonald's** on Yonge St. just north of College, about the half-way point, and the **Sicilian Ice Cream Parlour** (712 College St., tel. 416/531–7716). Around Christmastime in Little Italy, you'll find marzipan treats in some of the bakeries and Italian holiday breads and cakes.

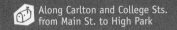

fruits and cafés in Little Italy. With the streetcar windows open, you'll catch the whiff of the scents and hear the sounds of a dozen languages. You'll also pass by some of the city's less affluent sections such as Regent's Park near Gerrard and Parliament.

You can hop off to visit some top family attractions along the way such as Riverdale Farm in Cabbagetown, the Toronto Police Museum and Discovery Centre on College Street, or High Park's Adventure Playground. All of these are free, and with a child's streetcar ticket costing 50 cents, it makes for an inexpensive outing that could last an entire day. There are few cities left who have their versions of the Red Rocket—San Francisco, Pittsburgh, and Mexico City to name a few. Though citizens may complain about the lumbering speed, the noisy rumblings, and the delays caused by the streetcars, your four-year-old will love getting a chance to see the city from this perspective.

KEEP IN MIND Did your kids have their noses pressed to the streetcar windows? Take them to the unique Halton Country Radial Railway (tel. 519/856–9802), Ontario's only operating streetcar museum, in Milton (about 45 minutes from Toronto). They'll be able to ride working historic models along a 2-km (1.2-mi) scenic track and climb aboard a replica of an 1893 open cable car. It's Canada's largest collection. The museum is open May–June, September–October, weekends and holidays 10–5; July–August, daily 10–4; $7.50 adults, $5.50 ages 3–18.

GARDINER MUSEUM OF CERAMIC ART

What would you do if your china collection was growing so fast that you were piling porcelain plates under beds and filling cupboards and drawers with earthenware figures? In short, your house was "choc-a-block full" with ceramics? George R. Gardiner and his wife Helen built a museum to house their collection and everyone is invited to come see it. The Gardiner Museum of Ceramic Art, one of the city's treasures, opened in 1984 as the first museum in North America devoted to ceramics.

Kids can grab a clipboard and a pencil from the bin at the first gallery's entrance to sketch any details or scenes that catch their eye—the funny masked face of an ancient Mayan pouring jug or an earthenware warrior from AD 950, the colourful Italian comedy figurines that amused 18th-century guests during dessert, or the ferocious dragons on blue-and-white Chinese porcelain. The more than 2,000 items include pre-Columbian

KEEP IN MIND If you're visiting near December, don't miss taking the kids to one of the city's special holiday traditions—the Twelve Trees of Christmas at the Gardiner. Each year, interior designers decorate the trees to show a theme, like Favourite Fairy Tales or Art Through the Ages. The bare evergreens might be covered with fairy dust and pirates from Peter Pan or Picasso-like ornaments. After two weeks of display, these magical trees are auctioned off to be set up at hospitals, offices, or in people's homes.

Note that the first Tuesday of the month is free.

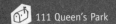 111 Queen's Park

416/586–8080

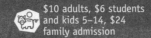 $10 adults, $6 students and kids 5–14, $24 family admission

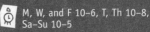 M, W, and F 10–6, T, Th 10–8, Sa–Su 10–5

 3 and up

earthenware figures dating from 3000 BC, modern-day plates, and crazy teapots. Little ones may need a stepstool. Older kids can follow the free audio guide that points out the museum's major pieces.

Special Family Sundays, held three or four times a year, offer musical entertainments, arts activities, and workshops. But every Sunday from 1 to 3 artists from 3 to 93 can sculpt animals, figurines, or dishes in the Clay Pit ($8 adults, $5 kids) with help from professional potters; a pottery wheel and kiln are available on site. You can pay a small extra charge for glazing and firing. The best is that if you don't finish in one session, come back as often as you like. It could be the start of a brand new hobby—or collection.

HEY, KIDS! The blue-and-white china in the cases on the second floor may seem all alike but look closely. What can you find? Artists not only painted pretty flowers and animals but also scary pictures of lions and dragons and men with swords riding horses. Can you find the dragon with a head of a bull, the eyes of a shrimp, the scales of a fish, the ears of an elephant, and the claws of a phoenix?

EATS FOR KIDS The museum serves lunch in its second-floor restaurant, **À la Carte Kitchen** (tel. 416/586–8080) but it might be better to treat a child to tea or a drink here as food service tends to be leisurely. In warm weather, have a snack on the outdoor patio. For a full-service meal, try **Mövenpick** (133 Yorkville Ave., tel. 416/926–9545) a few blocks north, where they greet kids with animal masks and crayons. Try "Big Bird's" chicken fingers or the "Pinocchio" burger. For a treat, visit **Greg's Ice Cream** just steps away (200 Bloor St. W., tel. 416/961–4734). Also see Royal Ontario Museum.

GIBSON HOUSE MUSEUM

What would life have been like for a child in 1851? At the rural, redbrick Georgian-style home of David and Eliza Gibson, the Gibson House Museum, it's easy to see. Much time was obviously spent doing chores such as churning butter, dipping candles to read by in the evenings, or dyeing sheep's wool in preparation for the spinning wheel. But the family also had fun making handkerchief dolls, baking derby cakes in the kitchen fireplace, or getting ready for Hogmanay, the Scottish New Year's celebration.

The charming two-storey house replaced the original farmhouse that was burned by government troops in retaliation for David Gibson's involvement in the Rebellion of 1837. Eliza escaped with her four children taking only her papers, her husband's tools, and the face and inner workings of their tall case clock. It sits today, refurbished and ticking, in the dining room.

KEEP IN MIND Costumed volunteers can show you around every day between 11 AM and 3 PM, but if you would like to visit earlier or later in the day, call ahead. The museum staff will arrange for a guided tour.

EATS FOR KIDS The house is hidden away, dwarfed by North York high-rises, but there are lots of eating opportunities nearby. At the Novotel Hotel across the street, **Café Nicole** (3 Park Home Ave., tel. 416/218–3868) has a children's menu; at **Indigo Books & Music** (5095 Yonge St., tel. 416/221–6171), a café serves peanut butter or grilled cheese sandwiches; and **McDonald's** (5200 Yonge St., tel. 416/224–1600) sits just north. The adjacent Gibson Park, worth a visit on its own for its quirky commemoration of the Gibson family (ask for info at the Museum), is a lovely place for a picnic.

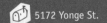 5172 Yonge St.

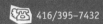 416/395-7432

 $2.75 adults,
$1.75 children 2-12

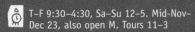 T-F 9:30-4:30, Sa-Su 12-5. Mid-Nov-Dec 23, also open M. Tours 11-3

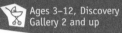 Ages 3-12, Discovery Gallery 2 and up

If there's a real sense of warmth and family here, it's no surprise. Seven Gibson kids lived here, then son Peter raised his 10 children in the home. Kids will be interested in seeing the youngster's small beds (where they slept in twos), the formal dining room with its funny long-tined forks, and the hired-man's room with the chamber pot conveniently under the bed.

On special days and weekends, kids can try some of the family tasks such as pounding the sugar for currant scones, turning whipping cream, sugar, and milk into ice cream, or playing old-fashioned games on the lawn. On most days, homemade soda bread and preserves welcome you in the kitchen. The small Discovery Gallery gives kids the chance to play early settler in a straw hat and vest or a pinafore, try carding fleece, or braiding a rug with strips of fabric. Even toddlers will find activities in the discovery bins, such as a felt board with farm animals.

HEY, KIDS! You may know about Christmas and Hanukkah but have you ever heard of Hogmanay? It's the Scottish celebration to welcome the New Year. At midnight, pots and pans are banged together to chase away evil spirits and everyone watches to see who will be the first person to step across the threshold into the house. He or she is called the "first-footer" and brings good luck. At the Gibson House on New Year's Eve afternoon, you can make noise makers, listen to stories, and try haggis (minced heart, lung, and organs of a sheep or calf, held together with sheep intestines and boiled!).

H.M.C.S. HAIDA

Discover life aboard Canada's most decorated naval warship, the H.M.C.S. *Haida*. Serving in both World War II and the Korean War, she helped to sink 14 enemy vessels in the Atlantic and to bombard Communist shore supply trains in Korea. This last remaining Tribal Class Destroyer is named after the aboriginal Haida tribe from British Columbia. The ship's badge displays a Thunder River Bird—Haida legend says that when a Thunder River Bird flaps its wings, thunder flashes from its eyes. Docked in the harbour alongside Ontario Place, the retired warship now serves as a maritime museum, a naval memorial, a national historic site, and an exciting place to explore with the kids.

There's a lot of ascending and descending on this self-guided tour—up narrow staircases and down steep ladders—but the ship is more than a glorified Stairmaster™. Visit the bridge and shout down the voice pipes to the Captain's Cabin. Descend below to the engine room or the mess deck where sailors lived, ate, and slept. Dotted about the ship are rather spooky-looking mannequins, swinging in hammocks, playing checkers in the Mess Deck,

HEY, KIDS! Did you know that H.M.C.S. stands for Her Majesty's Canadian Ship? The gift shop sells a video all about the H.M.C.S. *Haida* and its history. But you can get a terrific sense of what it would be like aboard one of these warships by watching a video called *The Cruel Sea*. You'll see the men sleeping in hammocks, the rough waters, the open bridge, the storms at sea, the submarine attacks, and the monotony when all was calm—just like life aboard the *Haida*. It's a great film based on the book by author Nicholas Monsarrat.

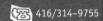
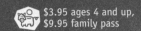
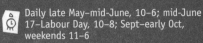

or getting ready to fire from the Transmitting Station. Some 200 young men served on the ship, making a home for themselves in this decidedly un-homey metallic hull. Every day, the noon gun is fired from the ship. On Saturdays, your kids can send a message in Morse Code from the vintage yet fully operational Radio Room. Learning to tap out their names, they'll get a certificate welcoming them to the Sparkers Club.

If you have a parent, relative, or friend who is a veteran, invite them along. Perhaps they'll be able to explain interesting details: the Christening Bell used as a font for babies, the open bridge that was freezing in northern climes, or the displayed newspaper headline that crows, "Sailors Enjoy Revenge as Nazis Flee Like Rats." It's a special history lesson for the kids when someone with actual experience explains the glories and the horrors of war.

EATS FOR KIDS

If Ontario Place is open, there are lots of fast-food choices next door or you can feast as a family at the on-site restaurant. Otherwise, you best bet is to eat before or after along Queen's Quay West. (see The Pier or Harbourfront Centre) or near Historic Fort York (see Historic Fort York).

KEEP IN MIND With no public washrooms onboard and only a portable toilet on site in summer, make sure the young sailors do toilet duty before boarding. If your kids feel the urge, you'll have to walk the distance to Ontario Place. On your tour, you'll be descending down steep ladders, up narrow staircases, and across suspended catwalks. This is no place for a stroller or a wiggly babe-in-arms. Also recommended: pants for mom who may not want to climb a steep ladder in a skirt. Note the tour is free with an Ontario Place Play All-Day Pass.

HARBOURFRONT CENTRE

I f you have to satisfy the far-flung interests of several children at once, this is the one-stop location for you. Where else in the city can kids paint a mural, swivel to salsa rhythms, watch a glassblower, sail a boat on a small pond, shop for hand-made clothes, attend an opera, and ogle some contemporary art, all in the same afternoon? Harbourfront Centre, one of Canada's leading contemporary cultural institutions, hosts some 4,000 events each year on its ten-acre, waterfront property.

Sunday is probably the liveliest day, when Cushion Concerts with professional performers, free world-beat music concerts (2–5 PM), and HarbourKids Creative Workshops (12–5 PM) are in full swing. On summer weekends, your kids can steer a remote-control yacht around the canoe pond ($5 for 15 minutes), or you can show them how to paddle like a Voyageur on the lake in a canoe rented from the adjacent sailing school. During the winter, the pond turns into Canada's largest outdoor artificial ice-skating rink (open daily, 10

43

EATS FOR KIDS
At the **LAKESIDE EATS** you can chow down on edible kid-pleasing fare. On a fine day, there's no better view than from the terrace. **Queen's Quay,** the shopping and eating emporium, is steps away. *See* The Pier for other good bets.

HEY, KIDS! If you like to make things with your hands, don't miss the Harbourfront Craft Studios. Standing on a kind of balcony, you can watch the crafts students as they work at their metal benches, blow glass, throw a bowl on the pottery wheel, or turn a piece of silk into a rainbow of colours with dye. You can see some of their final products in Bounty, the craft shop at Harbourfront. Don't feel shy about asking any questions. The crafters were once like you—beginners at their craft—and part of their job is to answer anything, no matter how silly. So ask away!

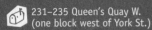 231–235 Queen's Quay W.
(one block west of York St.)

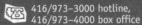 416/973–3000 hotline,
416/973–4000 box office

 Free, $2 workshops,
$8 Cushion Concerts,
some performances extra

 Daily 10–6. Cushion Concerts Oct–Apr, Su 1.
Marketplace early June–early Sept, F 6 PM–
midnight, Sa 11 AM–midnight, Su 11–7

 All ages. Cushion Concerts
5–12, workshops 3–12

AM–10 PM, tel. 416/973–4866) with music, lights, and hot chocolate. There are changing rooms, rentals, sharpening services, and lessons even for adults.

Harbourfront's programing draws on the city's multicultural atmosphere. Depending on the season, you can help celebrate Brazil's birthday, learn how to cook hot and spicy Indian food, make Japanese origami birds, attend an aboriginal drumming workshop, or celebrate Swedish Christmas with young girls wearing crowns.

With two art galleries, three theatres, two outdoor stages, a marina, a crafts studio, a pond, the terrific Soulpepper Theatre Company (offering a Bring Your Parents price for kids under 19), and a boardwalk along the lake, there is something for everyone. In summer months, your older kids can browse the weekend International Market. And everyone enjoys the movies under the stars in August.

KEEP IN MIND Top-notch family festivals include the world-renowned Milk International Children's Festival of the Arts in May—150 performances of music, theatre, dance, and puppetry from 6 continents—and the Toronto Festival of Storytelling in February with legends, songs, and stories from around the world. First Night Toronto!, rings in New Year's Eve early with 400 performances and 50 shows. The October HarvestFest on Thanksgiving weekend could present a Wild West show, pumpkin carving, or pony rides; Kuumba celebrates African Heritage Month in February.

HAUNTED KENSINGTON & CHINATOWN WALK

Tour guide Shirley Lum begins her walk with the spooky question: "Toronto means meeting place in the First Nations language. But is it a meeting place for the living—or for the dead?" Standing under the black cat sculpture at the tour's starting point, Lum tells stories of hauntings and strange happenings in the surrounding buildings. As you stroll the Kensington Market and Chinatown neighbourhoods for more than two hours, you'll hear about more ghostly tales and imaginary sightings. As dusk falls and bats begin to swoop about in the garden of the last stop of The Grange, you wouldn't be surprised to see your dead uncle Max right in front of you.

Lum is a great storyteller as are all her guides and the tours are a mix of history and ghost accounts. Did you hear about the house in the formerly Jewish Kensington Market where the ghost cooked chicken soup in the basement? Or the story of 1920s revolutionary Emma Goldman being seen in the washroom of a Chinese restaurant? As you walk about

KEEP IN MIND Shirley Lum's company, A Taste of the World, offers other neighbourhood walks and bicycle tours good for families. How about "Ghosts, Greasepaint & Gallows," a walking search for the ghosts of the grand theatres or the "Cool Sundae Bike Tour" that celebrates the anniversary of the invention of the ice-cream cone? Of course, you dismount for gelato at the Sicilian Sidewalk Café. Some teen fashion queens, for instance, would approve of the "Kensington Market Roots Walk" (a tour of Toronto's bustling street market) with stops at a vintage clothing shop and a discount designer's clothing store.

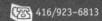
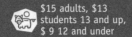

the streets—and there is a lot of walking—you'll not only learn about ghosts and spirits but also about Chinese culture and tradition, the history of Toronto, and the first immigrants. Along the way, you'll stop to sample the kinds of foods Chinese people bring to the cemetery to honor the dead, observe the octagonal mirrors to ward off evil spirits and ghosts, and learn the meanings of masks and mayhem.

If your adolescent has a lively imagination and is already a bit skittish, the ghost walk experience could provoke some anxiety. But if your children are into TV shows like *Buffy the Vampire Slayer* and *Charmed*, and gobble up mystery stories like popcorn, then they'll be all ears on this walk, get a bit of exercise, and learn some history in an attention–grabbing if somewhat scary way.

HEY, KIDS! Toronto is supposedly filled with ghosts. Famous haunted landmarks include Historic Fort York, the Gibraltar Point Lighthouse on Centre Island, and the home of Toronto's first mayor, William Lyon Mackenzie (Mackenzie House). John Robert Colombo's book *Haunted Toronto* has some more tales to creep you out.

EATS FOR KIDS After hearing the ghost story of the **Bright Pearl Seafood Restaurant** (346–348 Spadina Ave., tel. 416/979–3988), you may have to test this wedding banquet–type eatery with over 150 dishes. **Famous Seafood & BBQ Restaurant** (484 Dundas St. W., tel.416/217–0167) serves boiled chicken with a delicious topping of oil, green onion, and ginger or whole roast pig pieces. Warning: kids may fight over the crispy skin. At the **Tung Hing Bakery** (428 Dundas St. W., tel. 416/593–9375), buy some almond cookies or custard tarts to take home.

HIGH PARK

41

Though High Park is in the city's west end, you might say that it's Toronto's Central Park. For it's here that the crowds come on weekends to fly a kite, visit the small zoo, splash in the wading or swimming pools, ride the Trackless Train, go for a nature walk, and get a dose of nature that will last them the entire week. Why this location? Much of it was originally the estate of surveyor John George Howard and his wife Jemima, whose Regency-style villa, Colborne Lodge, sits at the park's south end. Howard asked that when they died (they are both buried on site), his land be turned into a public park.

It's terrific that some of the 300 acres (160 hectares) is so wild that there are signs not to feed the coyotes! There's a rare savanna of black oak trees, wildflowers, and nature trails leading to Grenadier Pond, certainly one of the most picturesque sights in Toronto. At the Children's Garden north of Colborne Lodge, you'll find family picnics on Sundays

HEY, KIDS!

It's easy to spot birds in High Park but keep your eye out for other wildlife. You might see toads or frogs by the pond, hawks circling overhead in fall, and scads of butterflies in late summer. At dusk, other creatures like bats or racoons appear. When you're tracking animals, be quiet, and don't wander off by yourself.

EATS FOR KIDS About midway through the park is **Grenadier Café and Teahouse** (tel. 416/769–9870) serving kids' portions of pizza, pasta, dino fingers (chicken fingers shaped like dinosaurs), and breakfast all day for $5.99. It's open 7–10 PM in summer, 7–7 PM in winter. Between May and October, there are two other options: the **Black Oak Café** booth at the northern entrance serves burgers, fries, and salads for outdoor tables. Near the Adventure Playground is a famous **snack bar** that serves fries, sausages, and burgers. The cook, George, braves the weather as long as park goers do. George cooks from 10–9 PM in summer, closing earlier in spring and fall.

 1873 Bloor St. W.

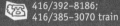 416/392–8186;
416/385–3070 train

 Free. Train $3 ages 13
and up, $2 children
2–12; nature walk $2

 Dawn to dark

 All ages

and gardening sessions on Thursday mornings (tel. 416/392–1560, ext 85695). There's a small zoo with pens of West Highland Cattle and llamas, but more enticing is the exciting Adventure Playground near the eastern gate. Built like a medieval castle, this climber offers ramps, slides, and swings. (A small fenced area is scaled down for preschoolers.) In spring and summer, ride the Trackless Train around the park.

In summer, take your teens to the annual Dream in High Park under the trees. The Shakespearian romps range from classic interpretations to gender-bending versions that go further than Shakespeare's original mix-ups. In freezing weather, Grenadier Pond becomes a natural skating rink. Sip hot chocolate or warm yourself by the outdoor fire. Better yet, if it's holiday time, sidle over to Colborne Lodge for cider and old-fashioned treats.

KEEP IN MIND Between April and November, you can join the High Park Walking Tours for families. On periodic Sunday afternoons at 1:15 and Tuesday evenings at 6:45, expeditions set out in search of bugs, butterflies, bats, and even faeries. Organized by citizens who are actively trying to restore the park's wilderness, the trips last a leisurely two hours. There's a final refreshment stop at Colborne Lodge (tel. 416/392–6916) for mint tea or raspberry fruit water (kids love it) and, if you like, a tour around the picturesque villa. Call tel. 416/392–1748 for the family nature walk schedule.

HIPPO AMPHIBUS

What's the hippest way to toodle around Toronto? Why in a Hippo Amphibus of course, a Canadian-made amphibious vehicle that does a 50-minute tour of the city, and then just like a hippo, splashes into Lake Ontario for a 40-minute float around the lake. Influenced by the World War II Ducks vehicle tours that are so popular in American cities like Boston and Chicago, Toronto Hippo Tours decided that their floating bus should be a hippo. It's an amphibian, it's purple, and it's fun.

The tour begins downtown, from the south side of the CN Tower on Bremner Boulevard. You'll pass many of the city's main attractions—the SkyDome, the Air Canada Centre, both the new and old City Halls, the theatre district, and the Princes' Gates at the Canadian National Exhibition grounds. Unlike the hop-on hop-off bus tours, this is an uninterrupted tour filled with historical information on the city and some trivia. Which famous comedians got their start at Toronto's Second City? Answer: John Candy, Eugene Levy,

HEY, KIDS! It's right that this bus should be called a hippo. The name hippopotamus means river horse, and even though it's a mammal, the hippo spends most of its time in the water. Most of the hippo's sense organs are placed along the very top of its head, so it can see, hear, and smell even if it's nearly completely under water. Hippos live in the rivers in Africa and come out at night to feed on grasses. Their babies learn to swim really quickly because they're born underwater and have to dive down under the water to drink milk from their mothers.

and Gilda Radner to name a few. Why are those people hanging off the walls at SkyDome? Artist Michael Snow wanted this gargoyle sculpture to represent everyone at the ball game—even the obnoxious screaming fans.

The highlight though is when the amphibus (which is actually a boat built around a yellow school bus) plunges into the water at Ontario Place. When the tour guide yells, "Do we want a little splash or a big splash?" your kids will no doubt scream "Big splash!" Sometimes, the water comes right over the top of the windshield. The Hippo floats among the other boats and travels under the building pods at Ontario Place. Then, like a Hippo, you can end the tour by emerging from the bus at Ontario Place for some sun on the Lake Ontario shore. Or you can travel back by land to where you began.

KEEP IN MIND The tours do hotel pickups on their first runs of the day. Around 9 AM, they'll start collecting passengers at the Toronto Colony Hotel or Metropolitan Hotel on Chestnut St., the Sheraton or Hilton on Richmond St., and the Marriott at the Eaton Centre.

EATS FOR KIDS Probably the best places to graze after riding the hippo are the restaurants around the SkyDome. At the **Hard Rock Café** (1 Blue Jays Way, SkyDome entrance by gate 1, tel. 416/341–2388), kids can order the Hippy Hippy Shakes or Joplin Juice to wash down Sergeant Pepper's Lonely Hearts Club Sandwich as they gaze at the autographed guitars and other rock 'n roll memorabilia. On the other side of the SkyDome is **Planet Hollywood** (277 Front St. W., tel. 416/596–7827) with movie memorabilia such as the white guitar from *Wayne's World* and California-style cuisine.

Historic Fort York is hidden away in Toronto's west end amid a tangle of expressways, street car lines, and factories near the Canadian National Exhibition grounds. But it's worth hunting out this small British fort, established in 1793 by Governor John Graves Simcoe on the Lake Ontario shore. The lake is no longer lapping up against the 1812 blockhouses and buildings—land was built-up south of the fort to anchor the Gardiner Expressway—but on many days, especially during the summer, the fort is peopled by soldiers and costumed guides who give tours and lead walks along the grassy fortifications.

The fort was never a major British defence post but one battle gives it great significance. On the morning of April 27, 1813, the settlement's 700 citizens woke up to find 14 heavily-armed American ships approaching the harbour. For six hours, 1700 soldiers tried to capture the fort for the U.S. before the British commander ordered the fort's magazine to be blown up. Hundreds of Americans were killed or wounded. The others

GETTING THERE Driving west along the Lake Shore Boulevard, turn north at Fleet Street and right onto Garrison Road toward the free parking lots. The fort is at the end of the road. By public transit, take the Bathurst streetcar south from the Bathurst station to the Exhibition Place Loop. It's about a seven minute walk up the hill.

EATS FOR KIDS Kids can chow down on hot dogs, sandwiches, pop, and ice cream bought at the fort's **The Canteen** snack bar, not exactly 1813 fare. The alternative is to bring your own fixings to the large lawn just outside the entrance. You might want to check out nearby trendy **Citron** (813 Queen St. W., tel. 416/504–2647) for its great Sunday brunch, or **Terroni** (720 Queen St. W., tel. 416/504–0320) for delicious, individual-portion pizza. There's a **McDonald's** close by at the corner of King St. W. and Spadina Ave.

looted and burned much of the town including the Parliament Buildings. In retaliation, British forces marched on Washington a year later and set fire to the President's Mansion. Myth has it that when the charred building was covered up with whitewash, it was then called the White House.

Your kids won't get to participate in this Battle of York (although they will get to watch a reenactment on special days) but on event days during the summer or March break, they'll be able to dress up like a soldier or an 1813 gentlewoman, march with a wooden musket to the drills of a gruff sergeant, or taste-test the goodies coming from the oven in the historic kitchen. More than 12,000 artifacts were found here during archaeological digs. Kids can view some of them, such as an American regimental button made from pewter through a magnifying glass. Guns brought by Simcoe over 200 years ago are also on display.

HEY, KIDS! Did you know that many kids lived at the fort in the early 1800s? If you were one of them, you would sleep in one bunk bed with about five or six other kids. You would only have two baths a year, and you would be bothered by two sorts of pests. One no longer lives in the city (rattlesnakes) but one certainly does (mosquitoes). But you would also have had fun running around the fort playing hide-and-seek and chasing the pigs that ran freely around the town.

HOCKEY HALL OF FAME

If Wayne Gretzky is the king of hockey, then this former Bank of Montreal building is the royal shrine to the game and to those who play Canada's favourite sport. And just like the sculptured bronze players positioned outside, poised to leap over the boards to begin (to play the game, not fight), so too can fans hardly contain themselves to step inside. On some days, there are long lines. Once inside, you'll notice a lot of grins from both young players and parents who remember those days on the ice.

Like a lot of games, the Hockey Hall of Fame is raucous and in your face, brash and interactive. In a rink-like area, try to stop Messier's and Gretzky's shots, test your slapshot against Hall of Fame goalies, become a play-by-play announcer, or watch movies of Gretzky's famous moments. Your kids may not be as interested in the historical displays—a 1960s family gathered in their "groovy" living room to watch "Hockey Night in Canada" or the first wooden ice skates. But the flashing lights, the displays of the

EATS FOR KIDS The Hockey Hall of Fame is perfectly positioned near some of Toronto's best family eateries. In BCE Place, impressive for its architecture, is **Marché Mövenpick** (42 Yonge St., tel. 416/366–8986) where kids can travel around to the various food stations and pick up pasta, fresh-squeezed juice, or scrumptious desserts. On some Sundays, between 10 and 1, a clown entertains the crowd. Just across the street is **Shopsy's** (33 Yonge St., tel. 416/365–3333), a family deli tradition. Its 15-page menu offers smoked meat sandwiches, dill pickles, and chocolate thunder cake for dessert among other kid-friendly choices.

30 Yonge St.

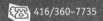 416/360-7735

$12 adults, $7 ages 4–18, $32 families, some extra charges

M–F 10–5, Sa 9:30–6, Su 10:30–5

4 and up

first goalie masks in honor of Jacques Plante, and the computers showing past Olympic Hockey games may catch their eye. As you tour the 16 zones dedicated to the sport, you'll see 57,000 square ft of hockey artifacts and memorabilia from the original organ from Maple Leaf Gardens to the recreation of the Montréal Canadiens dressing room.

It's only when you get upstairs into the marbled bank building with its stunning stained-glass ceiling dome and huge vault that the atmosphere quiets down, perhaps in reverence to North America's oldest trophy for professional athletes. The original Stanley Cup is on display in the vault, and everyone can see, touch, and even kiss the one that travels with the winning team. You can pay for a souvenir photo of this once-in-a-lifetime shot!

KEEP IN MIND Don't forget your camera for some great photo opportunities. Have the kids pose with the bronze players outside or let them hug the Stanley Cup. If you've got hockey-playing daughters, there's an encouraging shirt in the gift shop: "Hockey, Invented by Men, Perfected by Women."

HEY, KIDS! Why is the Stanley Cup called Stanley and not Howard or Frank? That's because it was named after Frederick Arthur Stanley, Baron of Preston and 16th Earl of Derby. In 1888, he became Canada's governor general, the Queen's man in Canada. But he was remembered more for donating the Stanley Cup to the country's greatest hockey players. The cup has been lost, misplaced, and even stolen since it was first awarded to the Montreal team in 1893. Maybe that's why they keep the original Stanley Cup in the bank vault.

JEWISH DISCOVERY PLACE
CHILDREN'S MUSEUM

Although Jewish Discovery Place is focused on teaching the history, customs, traditions, and values of Judaism, any child from any religion or background is welcome to explore the wide-open room. This special children's museum, the first of its kind in Canada and second in North America, is within the Bathurst Jewish Community Centre. The hand-on activities reflect Jewish traditions and offer endless possibilities of imaginative play in a busy, colourful environment.

At the re-created "Wailing Wall," kids can write a wish and post it to their Maker. Young bakers pretend to bake the Friday-night challah bread in the pint-size play kitchen, and imaginative travellers can "fly" to Israel in the small, realistic-looking airplane. A cosy place is the curtained dark room where Jewish symbols glow in the dark along with star constellations. The dollhouse here is a synagogue with a miniature rabbi,

KEEP IN MIND You can make a day of it at the Bathurst Jewish Community Centre and enjoy the large outdoor swimming pools. Day pool passes cost $10.70 for adults, $5.35 for 15–17, and $5 for 5–14. Check for free swim times (tel. 416/636–1880, ext 252).

HEY, KIDS! In the "Windows on our World" exhibit, you can listen to video messages sent just to you. Lift the tiny doors to hear words of wisdom from famous people such as Mel Lastman, the Mayor of Toronto, musical superstars such as Sharon, Lois, and Bram, and important businessmen like "Honest" Ed Mirvish. They each had only a few minutes to record a tip for kids, like looking both ways before you cross the street, always be on time, or when you're sad, make something. What tip would you give to kids if you could be behind a door?

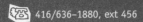

the tree-house-like climber is Noah's Ark—lie down under to listen to a story from Noah's wife—and the crafts may be influenced by Hebrew letters or Old Testament tales. The universal themes such as caring for the animals, sharing with your family, or helping the sick appeal to all ages, and kids will pick up on this faster than many adults.

During the summer months, workshops are held daily at no extra charge, usually in the early afternoon, when kids can create musical instruments for songs, listen to stories, or play games like Jewish Twister. The tables and chairs are kid-size; even toddlers will feel at home. You must stay with your children while they play here but that's no problem. You'll probably have as much fun as them, trying to fit in as many activities as possible.

EATS FOR KIDS The lobby's **Second Cup** coffee stand serves muffins, cookies, and drinks; the cafeteria run by **Rachel's Catering** (tel. 416/633–6661) cooks family buffet breakfasts, lunches, and dinners from 7 AM. At nearby **Bagel Plus** (634 Sheppard Ave. W., tel. 416/635–9988) you can take-out or eat-in Jewish deli food including some of the city's best bagels. Just below Sheppard Avenue is **Earl Bales Park** (4169 Bathurst St., tel. 416/395–7873), where you can barbecue hot dogs as well as hike the trails.

KAJAMA TALL SHIP

Have you ever dreamed of sailing aboard a tall ship, hair blowing in the wind as the seven sails catch the breeze? Or how about helping to hoist the mainsail or steer? In Toronto, the recently refurbished *Kajama* schooner provides that experience with 1½- to 2-hour trips out to the Toronto Islands and beyond.

Originally launched as the *Wilfried* in 1930, the 165-ft three-masted schooner was a familiar sight in ports from northwest Spain through western Europe and as far north as Norway and Russia. For a time, it sailed under a Danish flag in the Baltic Sea carrying grain to Scandinavian breweries. In 1999, the Great Lakes Schooner Company bought the ailing *Kajama*, and motored it across the Atlantic to Toronto, where it refurbished the ship with new steel and outfitted it with new decks and rigging to the tune of a million dollars. Luckily, they had found the original drawings still at the shipyard, so they were able to accurately reconstruct the vessel to its former glory.

KEEP IN MIND Bring along warm clothes, even on a sunny summer day. Once out on the open water, the weather can turn breezy and cool. Unless it's storming, the ship sets sail so if the weather looks doubtful, take raincoats and umbrellas so you don't have to sit down below (although there are windows to observe the passing scene). Also recommended— flat rubber-soled shoes, as the deck can become slippery with Lake Ontario spray. And of course, sunscreen. If you want your child to wear a life vest, alert the crew. They'll find a suitable size vest.

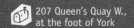 207 Queen's Quay W.,
at the foot of York

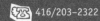 416/203–2322

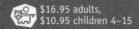 $16.95 adults,
$10.95 children 4–15

 Departs M–F 1 and 3; May–late Sept
also Sa, Su 11:30, 1:30, and 3:30

 All ages

The voyage begins with a short talk on safety. Then the large ship pushes off toward the lagoons of the Toronto Islands. An exciting moment is when the crew leap down several feet to pull on the rigging so the sails can rise up to catch the wind. There are not a lot of awesome sights to see as the ship glides beyond the Toronto harbour, so kids who may be bored with scenery—the island beaches, the Leslie Street Spit with its colonies of birds, and the cargo ships depositing loads at the industrial wharves—should bring along a book or other quiet activities. The drill onboard is to sit back and relax—there is comfortable seating for up to 165 passengers—and enjoy the temporary escape from life on land.

HEY, KIDS! If you want to help the Kajama crew sail the ship, just let them know when you board. The sailors, dressed in grey T-shirts, will show you how to pull the ropes, steer the ship, and maybe even how to swab the decks!

EATS FOR KIDS There's a snack bar onboard and drinks are served. Or if your crew makes up 10 people, the crew of the *Kajama* will pack box lunches, starting at about $10 per person (order in advance). It's easy, though, to eat at any of the restaurants at Queen's Quay (See *Harbourfront Centre* or *The Pier*) either before or after a sail. The other option is to make it a day on the water and book a brunch, lunch, or dinner cruise aboard one of the other boats that plies Toronto's harbour, like the Mariposa Cruise Line's ships (tel. 416/203–0178).

KORTRIGHT CENTRE FOR CONSERVATION

The Kortright Centre for Conservation is Canada's largest environmental education centre. That may sound dry and studious but it's anything but for kids. Yes it does have rooms where school classes dutifully take notes. But most of the education takes place in the great outdoors, no matter what the season. In spring, families can fly kites in the fields; in summer, take a walk on the wildflower side or follow the Honey Bee trail to the apiary and taste fresh honey. Fall brings foliage hikes through the woods and hawk watches, and if the snow piles on, there are sled dog races or cross-country skiing along 8 km (5 mi) of ski trails. Come dressed for whatever the weather as there is always something happening in this 800-acre (324-hectare) park.

Most of the action centres around the 16 km (10 mi) of trails that wind through the scenic valley of the Humber River. At 1 PM on weekends, you can join a 45-minute family

GETTING THERE Drive north on Highway 400, turn west at Major Mackenzie Drive (Exit 35), then south on Pine Valley Drive.

KEEP IN MIND With over 100 activities scheduled each year, it could be a wise investment to purchase a $30 Kortright Pass. This allows you unlimited admission (for two adults and two children 14 years old and under) for one year plus 50% reduction for events such as the Sugarbush Maple Syrup Festival. A $99 Conservation Journey Membership gives you access to all of the conservation areas in the Toronto area such as the Credit Valley Conservation Area or Nottawasaga.

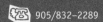

9550 Pine Valley Dr.

905/832-2289

$5 adults, $3 students and children 4 and up

Daily 10-4

All ages

hike led by naturalists. You might trek through forest, meadow, or marsh but it's always geared for young explorers. Ages 4 to 10 can also participate in craft projects—make a pinecone bird feeder or a kite out of balsa wood, paper, glue, and string. At any time, ask for a detailed map and set out on your own self-guided trail experience. Follow the Bird Feeder Trail marked with what else—30 bird feeders—or during the holiday season, the Christmas Folklore Trail when candle lanterns line the path.

The Visitor Centre offers interactive displays, fish tanks, and stuffed birds. But it's the unique programs that are the real draw. How often do you get to tour a sugar bush by lantern light, stroke a small brown bat, or talk to a beekeeper? Owl prowls, full moon campfires, bat nights, or migratory bird walks—when you mix kids and nature together in such an inventive and way, it works!

HEY, KIDS! The Kortright Centre has some really neat workshops for kids. How about the "Magic of Harry Potter Workshop for Would-Be Wizards"? You'll learn to look for magic in nature, see replicas of Harry's famous racing brooms, and plant a cutting for a whomping willow. Moms and dads might like the energy workshops that teach how to harness the power of the wind or the sun. These workshops are free with your admission but call ahead to register. You can check out what's happening at this busy nature center on their web site, www.kortright.org.

LILLIAN H. SMITH LIBRARY

This whimsical library building near University of Toronto was named after Canada's first trained children's librarian, who in 1922 created the first children's library in the British Empire in Toronto. Her Boys and Girls House became beloved by parents and children.

Bronze griffins guard the door to the library's new home, which was designed by architect Philip Carter to look like a medieval castle. Inside, curving steps and candlelike lamps lead down to a basement "dungeon." Like a castle, the library holds two special treasures—the Osborne Collection of Children's Books on the fourth floor, and the Merril Collection of Science Fiction, Speculation, and Fantasy on the third. You can't take out any of the treasures, but you can read them on site with your kids. (Toronto residents can borrow books from other floors with a Toronto library card.)

The original Osborne Collection of 2,000 books came from Derbyshire, England, in 1949—a sign of how deeply Lillian Smith's work impressed visiting librarian Dr. Edgar Osborne.

HEY, KIDS! You might be afraid to handle a 200-year-old children's book. But ask to see the reproductions of famous old children's stories that were published by Japanese book lovers. You can read such classics as *Puss in Boots* from 1897 or the 1856 *History of Robinson Crusoe*. At the Merril Collection, named after science fiction writer and editor Judith Merril, you can look at everything from the Buck Rogers comic books to the first edition of *Dracula*. But be careful! Some items may be the only known copies.

239 College St.

 Free

 M–Th 10–8:30, F 10–6, Sa 9–5, Su 1:30–5. Collections M–F 10–6, Sa 9–5

416/393–7746

3 and up

Added since are the Canadian Collection (children's books published since 1910). Ask to see a 1566 edition of *Aesop's Fables*, the earliest written version of *The Story of the Three Bears* (beautifully illustrated with watercolours), letters from Beatrix Potter, or nursery books given to Queen Mary by her Aunt Victoria. The collection also mounts intriguing book-related exhibits on trains, butterflies, and bees, or, in honour of the character Harry Potter, on wizards and magical creatures.

Sci-fi and fantasy lovers can delve into the 32,000 books, 25,000 periodicals, and role-playing games at the Merril Collection, one of the top-five collections of its kind in the world. Originally known as the "Spaced-Out Library," this noncirculating collection includes books on UFOs and legends of the mythical Atlantis.

KEEP IN MIND

Even if you are not a Toronto resident and eligible for a library card, you can check out www.tpl.toronto.on.ca for tips on parenting as well as lists of recommended books to read aloud. The Kids' Space offers stories, games, and tips on homework projects. In the collections, children under 10 should be accompanied by an adult.

EATS FOR KIDS At the corner of College and Spadina is a Burger King and a Mr. Sub but the funky places on west College Street are more interesting. At the no-frills **Mars** diner (432 College St., tel. 416/921–6332), kids can dine on food from the '50s—staples like rice pudding, muffins, and triple-decker sandwiches—served by mothering waitresses. Further along is the **Lava Restaurant and Nightclub** (507 College St., tel. 416/966–5282) offering '70s lava lamp action with ribs for teen sci-fi fans. It opens for dinner at 5:30 PM.

MCMICHAEL CANADIAN ART COLLECTION

Under the pine trees north of Toronto seems an unlikely place for one of Canada's most important art galleries. But this building—made of wood, stone, and glass—was once the home of a couple who collected artwork that reflected the rugged landscape of trees, rock, and water. In 1965, they donated their 10-acre property, home, and collection of 194 paintings to start a gallery devoted to the Group of Seven painters and other 20th-century Canadian art.

If you child has never been to an art gallery before, let this be the place to start. It's not your typical hush-hush space where if you stand back to look at a painting, you step on somebody's toes. Rather, it's a spacious, family-friendly place with high ceilings, scenic windows, hands-on joint art activities, and a unique collection of Canadian, Inuit, and First Nations art. The atmosphere is exuberant and the art is often bold—like depictions of blue snow against a purple sunset or the golden orange leaves of a forest, carved totems and Inuit sculpture, pioneer prairie scenes, and colourful native art.

GETTING THERE Follow the Don Valley Parkway north to Hwy 401 westbound; at Highway 400 go north to Major Mackenzie Drive West. Continue to Islington Avenue; the museum is just north.

HEY, KIDS! The Group of Seven artists modelled themselves on the Impressionists, the 19th-century artists in France who were fascinated with the ways colours changed outdoors at different times of day or season. Because these Canadian painters travelled to wilderness areas like Ontario's Algonquin Park to paint, they not only had to carry their art materials—portable sketch boxes, linseed oil or turpentine, cloths and brushes—but also a wooden canoe, a canvas tent, woolen clothing, metal dishes, and canned food. You can see a photo of one of their outings in the gallery. Quite an expedition to paint the autumn leaves!

 10365 Islington Ave.

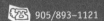 905/893–1121

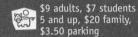 $9 adults, $7 students 5 and up, $20 family, $3.50 parking

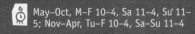 May–Oct, M–F 10–4, Sa 11–4, Su 11–5; Nov–Apr, Tu–F 10–4, Sa–Su 11–4

 4 and up

A good time to visit is Sunday from 1 PM until closing when the Drop-In Studio has art activities for all ages. For example, you might be encouraged to try landscape painting after seeing the West Coast paintings by Emily Carr, or you could carve a plaster bird inspired by Inuit carvings. The gallery hosts annual family days and hands out activity booklets for special exhibits. Kids are definitely welcome here and even asked to leave notes for the artists.

Part of the beauty of this gallery is its magnificent setting. Trek through some of 100 acres of woodland past wildflower meadows, sculptures, and the gravesites of most of the Group of Seven. Not only was the gallery recently voted Ontario's Best Indoor Site by Attractions Canada, but the kind of stunning nature depicted on the canvasses inside is available just outside the door.

EATS FOR KIDS The **Trailhead Café** outside serves hot dogs and ice cream but you might be better to bring your own outdoor picnic. Your teens may enjoy lunch or Sunday brunch at the elegant **Tanglewood** restaurant (tel. 905/893–0344, ext 402) overlooking the ravine while your little ones will love **Mr. McGregor's House Tea Room** (10503 Islington Ave., tel. 905/893–2508) in nearby Kleinburg. Decorated with Peter Rabbit cutouts and drawings from the Beatrix Potter books, the eatery offers homemade soups, sandwiches, and hot scones from the buffet dessert table.

NATHAN PHILLIPS SQUARE

In New York City, it's neon-lit Times Square; in London, it's pigeon-packed Trafalgar Square. In Toronto, the hub of human traffic is Nathan Phillips Square, named after Toronto's first Jewish mayor who served on the city council for 36 years. Here, outside Toronto City Hall, citizens gather for rock concerts and rallies, feasts and festivals, or just to while away a sunny afternoon by the reflecting pool fountain, skate on the rink (tel. 416/392–1111), or take photos of the city's famous black squirrels scurrying around the patches of grass.

It's fun to wander around the square discovering the curiosities—a Speaker's Corner on the south end dedicated to free speech where few take the opportunity to exercise it (Toronto's real Speaker's Corner is the video booth outside the ChumCity TV building); a Roman column on the north end, quarried in Egypt between AD 300 and 400 and given to Toronto by the Mayor of Rome; a fierce-looking Winston Churchill statue; Henry Moore's *The Archer* sculpture; and the calming Peace Garden, where Pope John Paul II

KEEP IN MIND Winter is also a great time at the Square, in December when the reflecting pool becomes a skating rink illuminated by more than 100,000 coloured lights and the 20-m (65-ft) Christmas tree is lit. Changing rooms, sharpening services, washrooms, a snack bar, and one of the largest underground parking garages in the world make this a convenient spot for a family skate. Each February during Winterfest, Inuit carvers arrive to chip ice and snow into dazzling sculptures. Don't miss the terrific skating shows on the rink, musical entertainment, and free pancake breakfasts.

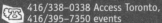 100 Queen St. W.

 Free

 416/338–0338 Access Toronto,
416/395–7350 events

Skating rink late Nov–mid Mar, daily.
Changing rooms 10–10

All ages

lit the peace flame with an ember from Hiroshima and poured water into the pool from the Nagasaki River.

During summertime, the square really comes to life. You may encounter farmers selling their wares, street performers, athletic competitors, and during Wednesday lunchtime concerts, rock musicians and salsa dancers. Kids' become part of the scene on Kids' Tuesdays when tables are set up between 11 and 1 for storytelling, face-painting, chalk art, and games. Call the events hotline to find out what's happening when. And who says kids don't count at City Hall? A playground for under sixes just west of Toronto City Hall is open between noon and 3 or whenever the on-site Hester How Workplace day care isn't using it. And if all this action gets to be too much, take the kids inside City Hall for a time-out story break in the small Public Library's children's section, near the windows on the first floor.

EATS FOR KIDS
At **Café on the Square** (Nathan Phillips Sq., tel. 416/861–0101), you might meet busy city politicians. In The Bay department store, the **Arcadian Court** (176 Yonge St., tel. 416/861–6611) is famous for chicken potpies.

HEY, KIDS! When Mayor Phillips wanted a new office, he held a contest for designs. When the new Toronto City Hall was opened in 1965, some said it looked like a space ship about to lift off. Others said it was a toilet with the lid down or a mistake because the towers were uneven. From an airplane, it looks like an eye. The space ship part is the pupil. But the architect who won the job from 520 entries, Viljo Revell from Finland, wanted it to look like God's arms protecting the earth.

ONTARIO PLACE

Ontario Place is a family amusement park with brains. Instead of shake-'em-up rides, you'll get exhibits on the human body or a whole room for Lego building. Instead of virtual reality, you'll find action-packed activities for toddlers (jumping into ball bins in the awesome Children's Village), for children (driving the Aquajet Racers), and for teens (riding the Wilderness Adventure Ride). No honky-tonk setting, the lovely park is built out onto the water with an atmosphere that's more in keeping with a fun, private yacht club. In fact, the operators are so sure your kids will have a good time that they are willing to guarantee "100 percent Good Clean Fun or your next visit is free."

Although you can stroll the grounds and partake of the free entertainment for $10, you'll probably want a Play All Day Pass for the kids. This gives them access to the grounds and dozens of rides and attractions including the Bumper Boats, the Megamaze (an indoor-outdoor labyrinth with seven ways in which to get lost), the Mini Greens golf, and the

EATS FOR KIDS There's a wealth of good eating choices here including a sit-down family restaurant. An outdoor food court offers the usual pizza and doughnut fare but you'll also find food booths serving ice cream and the like on the grounds.

KEEP IN MIND There are some shady areas—the Children's Village, for example, is under a giant tent—but because you're right on the lake, the sun can be glaring. Make sure you bring hats and sunscreen. Although the park is only open from May to Labour Day, the Cinesphere is open year-round. It's a treat to see IMAX films like *Mt. Everest* or Hollywood classics like the *Sound of Music* or *Back to the Future* on the six-storey giant screen. The price is right too: IMAX films are free with the Play All Day Pass; Hollywood films are only $6.

955 Lakeshore Blvd. W.

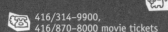416/314-9900,
416/870-8000 movie tickets

$10 ages 4 and up; free after 5 PM. Day Pass $24.50 adults and children over 106 cm; $11 children 4 and up under 106 cm; Night Pass 5-9, $10 for 4 and up

Mid-June–Labour Day, 10-9; mid-May weekend, Labour Day, and late-May–mid-June, daily 10-6, waterpark 10-4

All ages

Thrill Zone arcade, as well as a Water Splash area with slides and squirt-'em-up pumps. For time-outs, take advantage of musical entertainment at the Festival Stage and the Island Club and see *Franklin the Turtle* or Maurice Sendak's *Little Bear*.

Ontario Place is known for some unique special events such as the three-week Symphony of Fire International Fireworks Competition in June and July, when countries compete by setting their blasts to music (waterfront reserved seating extra). There's also the International Sandsculpting Competition. You can attend a concert at the Molson Amphitheatre featuring superstar musicians (admission extra), travel to Mars on a simulator ride, see an IMAX film on dolphins, or rent a canoe for a paddle around the pond. And all within arm's distance of the fresh cooling breezes from the lake.

HEY, KIDS! There's something here that you wouldn't usually find in an amusement park. It's the Japanese Temple Bell that sits in a little shingled house of its own under the evergreens. It's rung twice a year—on New Year's Eve and on Obon, a Buddhist remembrance day for relatives no longer living—but you can ring it too when you visit.

ONTARIO SCIENCE CENTRE

The Ontario Science Centre may sound potentially dull and boring—perhaps a think tank for governmental professor types—but it's anything but. For 30 years, kids have been coming to this nature-surrounded facility only to discover that science equals fun. With interactive activities ranging in theme from space to sports, from medicine to music, this giant play space for all ages has become a model for science centres around the world.

Have some priorities in mind before tackling the more than 800 hands-on exhibits in 13 halls. Do you want to steer an Olympic bobsled down a track or ring the bells from an Asian temple? Listen to a heart murmur or or play a new computer game? Probably the number one crowd-pleaser is the electricity workshop where kids can literally make their hair stand on end thanks to a Van der Graaf generator. Don't forget the camera!

KEEP IN MIND With one million visitors each year, the Science Centre gets crowded at times, and the noise level reverberates around the halls. It's best to go early in the morning or after 3, when the school or camp buses depart. Weekends are less crowded. If you like science museums, consider becoming a member of the Ontario Science Centre ($90 for one or two people over 16 and their kids or grandkids 17 or younger). The bonus? You'll get free admission to 199 science centres worldwide and discounts on workshops, programs, and events as well as half-price OMNIMAX movie tickets, half-price parking, and express check-in.

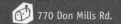 770 Don Mills Rd.

 $12 adults, $7 ages 13–17, $6 children 5–12

 Daily 10–5

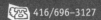 416/696–3127

All ages

The fun is not just for kids though. As you tour the busy halls, you'll be hard pressed not to jump onto a bicycle to see how much horse power you can generate, or navigate your way to the Moon on a rocket chair. As the staff says, "Have a little fun with that grey matter." At special workshops or lectures you might learn how to trace your family history or pose questions to a wolf expert. Changing exhibits could examine the science of roller coasters or present perfectly perplexing puzzles. Check the Internet site, www.osc.on.ca to see what's on or to sign up for special day outings or summer camps. For some temperamental types, the Centre might even be too stimulating. You might have to pace your visit with lots of breaks or a time-out lying on the floor in the small Planetarium to watch the star show. For others, the Centre is, according to at least one 11-year-old, "the most awesome place in the world."

GETTING THERE Take the Don Valley Parkway and follow the signs to Don Mills Road North. The Centre is on Don Mills Road just south of Eglinton. By subway, take the Yonge Street line to Eglinton station and then the 34 Eglinton East bus. Get off at Don Mills Road. Or, take the Bloor Street line to Pape Station and the 25 Don Mills bus north. Get off at St. Dennis Drive.

EATS FOR KIDS You have two choices for lunch. **Galileo's Bistro** (tel. 416/696–2484) serves hot buffet lunches with kids' prices and overlooks the ravine. Head to the basement level for the **Valley Marketplace Restaurant** (tel. 416/696–2483) with cafeteria-style pizza, sandwiches, grilled burgers, and the like. For snacks, there's a coffee booth at the entrance with sandwiches and drinks. If it's a nice day, take advantage of the natural setting for a picnic. There are a few outdoor tables just outside the restaurant or find your own secluded spot in the wetlands.

PARAMOUNT CANADA'S WONDERLAND

Paramount Canada's Wonderland is everything a big amusement park should be and more. With over 200 attractions and 60 rides, the park offers toddler's rides, playful characters, professional entertainment, special days devoted to families or multicultural festivals, a 20-acre water park, as well as the continent's largest assortment of roller-coasters—12 at last count. To celebrate its 20th season, designers added a water-soaking swing called Cliffhanger, Scooby-Doo's Haunted Mansion for the pint-size set, and Canada's only volcano—Wonder Mountain, which erupts all summer with a 10-minute display of fire, smoke, ash, and lava.

Of course, with this magnet of attractions come the crowds—over three million visitors a year. Try to come early or before the summer season to avoid the waits. Younger kids will head to the gentler rides at Hanna-Barbera Land or to Kidzville where parents ride along too. Both can test the Ghoster Coaster and take a photo with Fred Flinstone, Barney, or Scooby Doo. Don't miss the playground area with mazes, slides, a ball

EATS FOR KIDS There are eateries throughout the grounds, but they're somewhat expensive. You can't bring food into the park, but you can bring sandwiches and drinks to eat in the picnic area just outside the entrance. Just remember to get your hand stamped to reenter the park.

KEEP IN MIND There are two infant care centres with changing tables, rocking chairs, and private nursing areas; strollers and wagons can be rented. Bring water, sunscreen, and hats, especially if you're going to spend time at Splash Works. To avoid tears from kids too short to ride, explain the height restriction policy beforehand. A bonus—Family Season Passes are valid at any Paramount park, so if you're going to be in Charlotte, NC, Richmond, VA, Cincinnati, OH, or Santa Clara, CA later in the summer, take your Canada's Wonderland passes along to take advantage of this investment in summertime fun.

 9580 Jane St.

 905/832-8131

 $42.99 ages 7 and up,
$21.49 ages 3–6,
$23.99 grounds admission,
$279.95 Family Season Pass

 May–June, Sa–Su 10–8; May, M–F,
10–6; June, M–F, 10–10; July–early
Sept, daily 10–10; Sept–early Oct,

Sa–Su 10–8

room, and musical performances. Older children will want to try everything so get set for a full day's outing, topped off by nightly entertainment. The height restrictions kick in at 40 in, 44 in, and 48 in, at which point your kids can ride anything they dare.

Splash Works (open at 11) is a park in itself with 18 water slides, a wave pool, a tube ride, and the Pumphouse. Every five minutes, a bucket of water spills onto the boisterous Pumphouse participants. Canada's Wonderland also plans special events throughout the season featuring stuntmen, magic shows, ethnic festivals, even a physics, science, and math day. The Magic School Bus or puppets entertain the youngsters during the day, and teens can catch shows like *Electric Circus—Live*, broadcast by MuchMusic, in the evening. Keep watch for new rides and attractions. It's a summer-long party that never lets up.

HEY, KIDS! Lines for the the 12 rollercoasters can get long, so you might want to be picky. You can loop the loop on Dragon Fire, stand up while riding Sky Rider, or rattle your bones on The Wild Beast, a wooden roller coaster. The Mighty Canadian Minebuster is the biggest in the park. Some say that Top Gun is the scariest. The Bat takes you backwards, and The Fly rides you longest. If you start feeling a little queasy, it's time to take a break.

THE PIER

The Pier, Toronto's Waterfront Museum, is smack dab on the harbour in a restored 1930 shipping warehouse. This small, family-friendly museum, dedicated to boats and the nautical history of Toronto, celebrates the important relationship between citizens and the bay. Although today you see mostly ferries and tour boats arriving at the harbour, all kinds of ships have plied Toronto's waters since its early days—from the canoes of the Native peoples and British schooners full of settlers, to the Great Lakes steamships picking up this century's passengers for trips to the northern woods. An oil painting here depicts Governor John Graves Simcoe and his wife Elizabeth arriving by schooner in 1793 to begin settlement of Toronto.

The film about Toronto's harbour from the time of "boggy marshes and rotten wharves" is best appreciated by older children. There's also plenty of information to read on Toronto's largest harbour disaster: a dock-side fire aboard the elegant *Noronic* carrying 550 passengers. But aside from looking at the dozens of ship models here, kids can blast

EATS FOR KIDS Continue the nautical theme at **Pier 4 Storehouse** (245 Queens Quay W., tel. 416/203–1440) behind the museum where kids can gaze at lobster traps, old shipping crates, and a fake shark while munching on fish and chips. You can order the lobster. In the Queen's Quay Terminal building (207 Queens Quay W.) past Harbourfront Centre is **Spinnakers** (tel. 416/203–0559), where you can sit outside to watch the boats, and **Pumpernickel's Deli & Catering** (tel. 416/861–0226), on the second floor. Lunch at the deli is inexpensive and hearty—just $2.50 for hot soup and a sandwich.

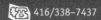
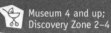
the real ship's whistles lined up in a row, such as the piercing model from a 1906 Toronto Islands ferry, try their hand at Morse Code just like a ship's wireless operator, or strain to outdo you as well as celebrated Ontario sculling champion Ned Hanlon on a rowing machine.

The newly expanded Discovery Zone has moveable tugboats and a costume corner where kids can dress up like sailors, pirates, or yachtsmen to "sail away" on a rowboat. Bring the camera to snap them in these wonderful outfits handmade by a professional costume designer. Older kids learn to tie knots or operate the small model canal system. For toddlers, a resting corner offers pillows decorated like semaphore flags and large blocks so that they can build their own "boats." Your family can also set out on Discovery Trail to find specific hidden treasures in the museum and receive a reward.

HEY, KIDS! Want to learn how to tap secret messages at the dinner table or through a bedroom wall? Learn some Morse Code communication skills at the Pier. How does it work? Short and long signals called dots and dashes represent letters or numbers. For example, number 4 is four quick dots and a long dash.

KEEP IN MIND If your kids are between the ages of 4 and 10 and love playing pirate, why not schedule a pirate birthday party at the Pier? Between 8 and 20 kids ($10 each) can dress up like Captain Hook, take the Pirates' Pledge, create their own pirate hats, sport eye patches and swords, and make a model of their very own ship. Not to worry about leaving the party without finding the buried treasure. Loot bags for each guest can be arranged for $3 each. To book, call 416/597-0965.

PLAYDIUM

Most kids' eyes light up when they walk into this lively, some might say, rocking emporium. The music's full blast, spotlights flash around the floors and ceiling, the games ring and ping, and the chrome and neon colours illuminate the darkness. The Playdium's doorway onto the street is relatively inconspicuous. But step inside the entrance and presto— the tunnel behind the cashier opens into a four-storey space that buzzes with high-tech action. There's no quietly reading a book while your young charges have fun here.

Some kids won't know what to do first. Will it be the Virtual Indy car race in the Sports Zone, a South Park pinball machine in Pinball Alley, or playing drums along with Santana in the Music Zone? There's a 40-ft crimson climbing wall, photo booths that morph humans into monkeys, and glow-in-the-dark air hockey tables. You may have to guide kids around with a firm hand and put a limit on how many of the 270 attractions they can try. Although some of the Kids Corner games cost only 25 cents, they're less than exciting compared

HEY, KIDS!

Do you, your friends, or parents have an e-mail address? If so, you can sign up to get e-mail news from Playdium. You'll hear about new games, special offers, or events. Just by sending your e-mail address to info@playdium.com, you'll get 20 Bonus PlayerOne points.

KEEP IN MIND On a budget? Save on Powerplay Wednesdays after 4 (3 hours of unlimited play for $22) or, with your teens, Midnight Madness Fridays after 10PM (4 hours of play for $25). For about $17.50 per person, a Family 4 Pack gives 120 credit points, about a $20 value, for a two-hour PlayCard, a hot dog or pizza and pop, and free parking in Festival Hall. A same-day movie stub from the Paramount movie theatre around the corner gets $5 off admission. Or sign up for PlayerOne Membership to earn credits with every dollar you spend.

 126 John St.

 Games 25 cents and up

416/260-1400

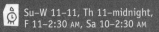 Su–W 11–11, Th 11–midnight,
F 11–2:30 AM, Sa 10–2:30 AM

 6 and up

to the big games that average between $1.50 and $2 a play. The costs can add up fast, especially with older kids who won't be content to sit in a zebra striped seat to watch the antelopes leap on a screen or to watch others (like you) play. You can fill your PlayCard with cash, a credit card, or Interac (an ATM machine); play unused credit on a future visit or at Playdium Mississauga (99 Rathburn Rd. W., tel. 905/273–9000) with its outdoor go-karts, mini-golf, and beach volleyball.

Weekends are busy with birthday parties (call ext 233 for enquiries), so try to visit before noon on Saturdays to avoid the crowds. In the evenings, teens take over. And if you want to steer clear of the wild shoot-em-up or combat type games, avoid the Target and Contact zones. Your kids can "virtually" hang glide, jet ski, sky dive, snowboard, play basketball, and catch a bass—all in one afternoon.

EATS FOR KIDS All that action works up an appetite. Grab a bite at the **Playdium Express** snack bar, or keep playing at the **Playdium City Diner** where booths are equipped with state-of-the-art television screens and cutaway video controls at each place setting. Chicken wings or salads can be viewed on screen before ordering. In the evening, the **Kasbar** comes alive. Sit in Moroccan style booths or on hassocks to order drinks or food. Kids accompanied by an adult can also eat in the **SportsBar** to watch sports on one of the biggest indoor screens in Toronto.

R.C. HARRIS FILTRATION PLANT

How does Great Lake water, filled with algae and fish, debris and dirt, turn into crystal-clear drinking water that comes out of your home tap? A guided tour around the R.C. Harris Filtration Plant, an imposing Art Deco set of structures overlooking the lake, will show you how. On a one-hour trip, you'll be led around the large humming pumping machines, through a pipe-lined tunnel, up an elevator into the Service Building, and into a darkened chamber shimmering with basins of filtered water. It's a fascinating journey.

"The Story of Drinking Water" cartoon booklet, handed out free to kids at the start of the tour, explains the process of adding chlorine to prevent bacteria, sulphur dioxide to reduce the level of chlorine, aluminum sulphate to clump together remaining harmful micro-organisms for removal, ammonia for extra purification, and fluoride to prevent tooth decay—in an easy-to-read format. At the end of this complicated process, the liquid is sent underground

KEEP IN MIND Children under 10 must be accompanied by an adult. Because this is a working plant rather than a tourist attraction, the smells of the chemicals and equipment and ongoing noise of large turbine machines may upset some kids. Some will love standing on a floor grate with water swirling underneath but some could be scared. Not to worry. If a child wants to leave, just outside is the beautiful green expanse of lawn and hills leading down to the lake, where there's a small beach.

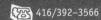 2701 Queen St. E.

416/392–3566

 Free

Tours Sa 10, 11:30, and 1 PM

6 and up

to reservoirs where it's pumped to thousands of homes. This plant produces almost half of the city's water requirements, filtering about 950 million litres (251 American gallons) of lake water each day. Tell your kids that's as if the city delivers about 350 million large pop (soda) bottles to its citizens each day.

The complex itself, dubbed the "Palace of Purification" by some because of its elegance, is almost as interesting as what's going on inside. Built between 1937 and 1941 and named for Rowland Caldwell Harris, Commissioner of Works for 33 years, the streamlined Art Deco palace was treated to imported Italian marble, brass fittings, skylit gallerias, and a magnificent clock whose dials indicate time, reservoir levels, and rate of filtration. Loved by movie directors for its atmosphere, the water treatment facility has provided the setting for many films including *La Femme Nikita*, *Robocop,* and *The X-Men*.

HEY, KIDS! Ask for the free pamphlet "25 Things You Can Do to Prevent Water Waste." Some you probably know, such as "Don't run the water while cleaning your teeth," but some you may not such as "Use a broom, not a hose, to clean sidewalks."

EATS FOR KIDS There are lots of restaurants along Queen Street (*see* The Beaches). At the eastern end near the filtration plant, the **Garden Gate Restaurant** (2379 Queen St. E., tel. 416/694–3605) is a famous Beaches institution. It's known by the locals as "The Goof" because their Good Food neon sign was missing its letter "d" for quite a while. It's from another age with juke boxes at every table. **Tejas** (2282 Queen St. E., tel. 416/694–2643) has good Tex–Mex food.

REDPATH SUGAR MUSEUM

Your kids don't have to know how raw sugar cane is transformed into sugar crystals to enjoy sweet treats. But after a tour of the small museum with curator Richard Feltoe, they'll have a new understanding of what makes their lollipops and gum balls taste so good. Surprisingly, sugar used to be viewed as a real food, good for digestion and for "giving vigour to old people." They'll also be impressed to hear that sugar was so valuable, it was locked away in strong boxes, a far cry from today's open shelves overflowing with candy. Sugar also has some strange uses—it coats video tapes and is used for breakable glass in the movies.

Because this is a working factory with 3,000 employees laboring around the clock to produce 2000 tonnes of refined sugar each day, you won't be able to see the actual refining process up close. But the museum gives a good idea with pictures, artifacts, and a take-home booklet that shows how the sugar cane is processed into white and brown sugar as well as confectioner's sugar or powdered fruit sugar.

EATS FOR KIDS Across the street in Loblaws is a **Take Me Marché** café (10 Lower Jarvis St., tel. 416/366-2557) serving hot and cold fare. For a fun meal in a caboose, try the **Town and Country Buffet Restaurant** (190 Queen's Quay E., tel. 416/368-8500); menu items are half price for kids.

KEEP IN MIND Although the museum has scheduled hours, be sure to call ahead. The curator sometimes is called away for meetings. There are no interactive exhibits here, and no freebie take-home samples to excite the kids. But a visit could promote some good discussions, like how historically slaves bore the brunt of labor-intensive sugar production. As some pictures show, the grueling work of cutting sugar cane was done by the people of the Caribbean, often enslaved or indentured to plantation owners. Not all of sugar's history is sweet.

95 Queen's Quay W.

  M–F 10–12, 1–3:30

416/366–3561

Free

7–13

Redpath has been refining sugar in Montreal and Toronto since the mid-1800s—that white bag of sugar with the red writing has decorated breakfast tables for decades—and the museum contains many curiosities. The story of sugar starts at the museum entrance with some rare aquatints showing sugar production in Antigua in 1820. Along with historical photos of the Redpath family and huge cones of sugar (as it used to be sold), there's a family love letter written three ways—across, down, and sideways to save paper—and a photo of the company's 50th anniversary in 1854. Point out the differences to your kids of the owner's grandson in a suit, and the young factory boys wearing suspenders and caps. A highlight for kids is the collection of wrapped sugar cubes from around the world, the miniature sugar trucks, and the fake iced cakes. It's enough to make you want to head home and bake a sugar-laden cake to eat together.

HEY, KIDS! Some know the Redpath Sugar Refinery only by the huge colourful whale mural on the triangular wall outside. It's called "Whaling Wall" and was painted by an American artist that goes by the name of Wyland. During the 1990s, he set out on a mission to paint more than 70 murals across North America. Why? He wanted to stress the importance of saving our oceans. Perhaps he picked this industrial spot because it's overlooking Lake Ontario water. The mural can remind us to think of ways to keep the lake water clean.

RIVERDALE FARM

Oinks, grunts, moos, and gobbles—they're all here right in the middle of the city. It's almost unbelievable that a turn-of-the-20th-century farm with a farm house, a Pennsylvania stone and timber barn, and pens of animals can be thriving just minutes from downtown office buildings. But then, this land has been home to creatures since the original Riverdale Zoo opened in 1894. When the more animal-friendly Toronto Zoo opened in 1974, those caged critters were moved. Today the typical Ontario farm with split-rail fences, gardens filled with wildflowers, and wagon rides is the ideal setting for a smattering of farm animals that seem to come from central casting.

You'll find Bella, the soft-eyed Jersey cow who has given birth to three calves, fat black pigs wallowing in the mud, large Clydesdale horses and Shropshire sheep, and a whole pen of crowing roosters. In the spring, new babies arrive. Your toddler will love peering

KEEP IN MIND As well as being an urban rural retreat, Riverdale Farm is an education centre. As soon as your baby is one month old, you'll be able to attend Parent & Preschoolers sing-along sessions. When he's three, you can do Parent & Young Farmer programs. Older kids can sign up for pottery classes (ages 6–12) or the Farmer's Garden Sprout Club (ages 8–12). Adults too are welcome to learn pottery, spinning, weaving, or Country Line Dancing .

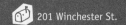 201 Winchester St.

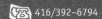 416/392-6794

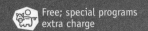 Free; special programs
extra charge

 Daily 9–4

 1–12

in at a dozen piglets fighting for mom's lunch or the baby lambs, wild and wooly. Often, the kids will be able to help with chores such as collecting eggs or feeding the animals. The buildings themselves are charming, especially the redbrick farm house (the original zoo keeper's home) and the high Pennsylvania Bank Barn donated to the farm in 1975.

Don't miss the lower areas where the Ponds Naturalization Project continues. In order to restore the wetland habitat, the area has been planted with native trees and the ponds stocked with amphibians. It's an exciting place for the kids to explore. There are lookout points, a small stone bridge, gravel paths for bikes or trikes (and an abandoned cage from Riverdale Zoo that looks like a cell from Alcatraz). You'll hear birds and bees, cicadas and crickets. If it wasn't for traffic noise from the nearby highway, you'd swear you were in the country.

HEY, KIDS! Did you know that pigs can bite? Or that the horses here have feathers around their feet? And why do pigs roll in the mud? Hint: it's so they won't get sunburnt. You can learn a lot by reading the signs posted around the farm.

EATS FOR KIDS The adjacent small park offers long tables and a lovely setting for family picnics or reunions. You can pick up drinks or snacks from the counter in The Simpson House. On the corner, **The Winchester Café** (161 Winchester St., tel. 416/924–4362) serves Sunday brunch 10–2 as well as full-course gourmet dinners Wednesday through Saturday from 5:30 PM. Its take-out window, **Window on the Park**, dishes up ice cream, muffins, hot dogs, and drinks for as long as the weather is warm enough.

ROY THOMSON HALL

Roy Thomson Hall, the city's shimmering glass concert building, is the setting for music of all kinds—Young People's Concerts on Saturday afternoons, Special Holiday programs for families, Toronto Symphony Orchestra Pops concerts, and songs from the Toronto Mendelssohn Choir. Informal, free, bring-your-own lunch sessions take place many Fridays at noon when young musicians perform in the lobby. And if your kids can't settle down for classical music, you can attend multimedia performances mixing music and film, military band extravaganzas, and cultural shows such as the Whirling Dervishes from Turkey. A symphony orchestra has even accompanied a screening of Bugs Bunny cartoons, and the Kronos Quartet has played to Bela Lugosi's *Dracula*.

The Young People's Concerts are the perfect introduction to the Toronto Symphony Orchestra for children 5 to 12. Presented on five Saturdays between fall and spring, these musical interactive journeys feature actors, children's authors and poets, kids' classical tales, and instruments that tickle the funny bones—from xylophones to zithers, flutes to

HEY, KIDS!

Think all you need are your ears to hear well? Not exactly. The way sound echoes around is called acoustics. To control these echoes, the seats, floor, and even ceiling tubes are covered with fabric. This way even a whisper travels easily to the back row (so be aware that everyone can hear the noise you make, too).

KEEP IN MIND Roy Thomson Hall has won awards for its consideration of people with special needs so it's a good venue for intergenerational get-togethers. There are 26 wheelchair locations on all levels for aging grandparents or for kids in wheelchairs and handicapped parking underground as well as accessible drinking fountains, telephone booths, and elevators. Ask at the House Manager's office for receivers for people with hearing impairments or for a complimentary back support. Call tel. 416/593–4828 or visit www.tso.on.ca to see if the Toronto Symphony is performing in a church or park near you, or even outdoors on the Toronto Islands.

 60 Simcoe St.

 416/593–4822 tours,
416/872–4255 tickets

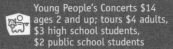 Young People's Concerts $14
ages 2 and up; tours $4 adults,
$3 high school students,
$2 public school students

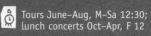 Tours June–Aug, M–Sa 12:30;
lunch concerts Oct–Apr, F 12

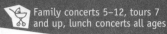 Family concerts 5–12, tours 7
and up, lunch concerts all ages

fiddles. Come early for a 20-minute informal preconcert session around the Yamaha piano that belonged to famous pianist Glenn Gould. The Pops Concerts also regale kids with music from *Star Wars* to funky jazz and blues.

The concert hall itself is worth a visit, especially for older kids who are interested in modern architecture, and summertime tours are conducted daily. When the honeycombed futuristic structure was first opened in 1992, there was an outcry over the monochromatic silver-gray colour scheme and its convex shape. But Canadian architect Arthur Erickson wanted the colours of the performers and the audience to take centre stage. On the 45-minute tour, your kids will get an appreciation of the design, discover if a whisper can carry 170 feet to the stage, and perhaps, if the orchestra isn't rehearsing, may even get to walk out onto the stage for an impromptu song debut.

EATS FOR KIDS Next door at Metro Hall, an underground food court has a **McDonald's** and other easy spots for families. Across the street is **Shopsy's TV City** (284 King St. W., tel. 416/599–5464) where 11 booths and tables equipped with Sony PlayStations should break the symphony silence. Handy for post- or pre-concert meals is a friendly eatery from the classic Italian chain, **Il Fornello** (214 King St. W., tel. 416/977–2855), which provides speedy service. Kids like the excellent pasta, minestrone soup, and individual pizzas baked in a wood-burning oven.

ROYAL ONTARIO MUSEUM

Don't even think about a quick in-and-out visit to Canada's largest museum. With 39,000 objects displayed in 39 galleries—everything from a three-storey West Coast totem to a superb Viking sword from AD 900, from a Northern Ontario moose to a rare Ming tomb—you can't possibly see it all in one day. If you're short on time, concentrate on the galleries popular with kids, interspersed with some quiet time in an out-of-the-way room where you can really look at that suit of armor built for a young German boy or examine the claws of a Chinese dragon sculpture.

The ROM has often been referred to as Canada's Smithsonian but directors prefer to consider it the country's treasure trove. Most enthralling for kids is the huge dinosaur collection, the Egyptian Gallery with its 2,500-year-old ancient mummies, and the re-created Jamaican Bat Cave with thousands of screeching bats (some are stuffed, but most are man-made). In the new Hands-On Biodiversity Gallery, kids can handle fur samples or

KEEP IN MIND If your kids want to visit the Discovery Gallery, ask for timed tickets at the entrance as soon as you arrive. Because there is a maximum number of kids allowed, the place fills up fast especially during school holidays. Between September and June, weekday mornings may be reserved for school groups so plan accordingly. The museum is free every day after 5, but beginning at 4:30 on Friday. The larger museum can be overwhelming for some small children. If you have kids ranging from babes to teens, you may want to split up with one parent taking preschoolers to the small Children's Own Museum next door (*see* Children's Own Museum).

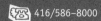 100 Queen's Park

416/586-8000

 $15 adults, $8 students and children 5–14, $35 family pass.

M–Th, Sa 10–6, F 10–9:30, Su 11–6

3 and up. Franklin's World 1–3

animal skeletons, tunnel under the earth to meet a fox in his lair, or pat Bruce, the live skink (a lizard with smooth, shiny skin) from Australia. Add facilitators who during holiday times organize scavenger hunts or roam the halls with live snakes, and you've got a friendly learning environment that's educational and exciting.

Your 5- to 12-year-olds won't want to miss the interactive Discovery Gallery. It's high stimulation as kids cruise through a crystal cave, dig for dinosaur bones, or try on chainmail headgear or hippie clothes from the '60s. Within pull-out drawers are projects requiring more concentration, such as reconstructing skeletons with real bones, or writing hieroglyphics. For four and unders, there's Franklin's World, named after the popular storybook turtle. Here, your preschoolers can crawl into an igloo to do puzzles or sit with you in a rocking chair for a story. Note that you must stay with any child younger than 10; those 10 to 12 must have a supervising adult in the museum.

HEY, KIDS! Although this is one of the country's oldest museums, it's cool because you can touch a lot of the exhibits. At the Hands-On Biodiversity Gallery, stroke a beaver pelt or handle a rough whale vertebrae. You can feel the rumbles of an earthquake with your hands at the Dynamic Earth gallery. Before you visit, you can surf over to *www.rom.on.ca* to find cool programs you'd like.

EATS FOR KIDS
For quick lunches, visit **Druxy's** (tel. 416/586–5563) on the main floor. Teens may appreciate the fourth-floor **JK ROM** restaurant (tel. 416/586–5578) overseen by top chef Jamie Kennedy. They'll get a great view of the city while munching some of the city's best french fries.

ST. LAWRENCE MARKET

I f you have babies or toddlers who get up early, very early, bundle them up and take them to the St. Lawrence Market for breakfast. Especially if it's a Saturday—the doors open at 5AM. You can smell the aromas from the sidewalks outside, but once in the South building, you'll encounter a riot of sights and sounds. Fishmongers hawk live lobsters and crabs from their tanks, butchers sell all manner of sausages and fowl, and cheese dealers slice off paper-thin pieces of Parmesan cheese from the humongous wheels of cheese. Within minutes, everybody's noses will be working overtime. Add in the musicians playing South American pipes or jazz saxophone, and craftspeople selling everything from Hawaiian shirts to hemp sweatshirts, and you've got a global shopping experience.

This corner has been dedicated to market produce for over 150 years. In the mid-1800s, as the city's first City Hall, the building was the place for meetings, concerts, and the farmer's market below. From the window of the Market Gallery (tel. 416/392–7604) upstairs

KEEP IN MIND Because the Market is so crowded on Saturdays, tow trucks are out in force towing illegally parked cars. Park at a meter or in a parking lot on the Esplanade so as to avoid a nasty surprise when you emerge with baby, stroller, and groceries.

EATS FOR KIDS Obviously, there are lots of places to buy snacks or sandwiches to eat on the picnic tables outside: peameal (a form of bacon with a rind) or Canadian back bacon at the **Carousel Bakery** (93 Front St. E., tel. 416/363–4247), veal and egg-plant at **Mustachio**, or barbecued chicken (best for kids) and custard tarts from **Churrasco St. Lawrence**. In wintertime, **Le Papillon** (16 Church St., tel. 416/363–0838) opens at 11 AM for crepes and hot chocolate. If your kids are grossed out by the strange market food, **McDonald's** (121 Front St. E., tel. 416/868–9998) or **Swiss Chalet/ Harvey's** (80 Front St. E., tel. 416/304–0826) should restore their appetites.

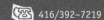 92 Front St. E.

 Free

Tu–Th 8–6, F 8–7, Sa 5–5; farmers'
market Sa 5 AM–6 PM ; flea market Su 11–5

416/392-7219

 9 and under

(the original council chambers, now an art gallery), you'll get a good overview of the action. As you stroll the halls, your kids will no doubt want to stop many times. The upstairs is huge, with stalls of butchers, fishmongers, cheese sellers, and bakeries. Downstairs are store-like booths, eating places, pasta specialists, and a spice market that will have even you baffled as to what to do with each item.

Across the road is the Farmers' Market (only open Saturday), where fresh products from the country are sold. It's fun to wander and to taste—chips and gourmet salsa dip from a countrywoman, green beans and herbs from a farm up north, or fresh goat cheese from a dairy farmer. You'll find honey and maple syrup, sausages, and strudel or chunks of chocolate. Ask your kids to help plan the evening meal based on what's available at the stands.

HEY, KIDS! The cheese shops here sell over 500 different kinds of cheese. You can ask for a sample to try some of them. The pasta bins hold dozens of different pastas—the colourful ones are made from tomatoes, spinach, and even squid ink. Have you ever had an Arctic char sandwich or seen an egg laid by an emu? It's almost like green eggs and ham! Some of these things may look strange but they are tasty. So be adventurous and try a new food.

THE SKYDOME

What's most surprising about SkyDome, Toronto's egg-shaped sports and entertainment stadium? Not its retractable roof nor its attached hotel whose rooms look onto the field, nor its spaceship-like aura when lit up at night. It's all the stuff the excavators unearthed when they were building it: a pocket spyglass, mustard jars and old bottles, bits of cannon and copper. You can see these archaeological finds on the SkyDome Tour Experience, a one-hour visit behind-the-scenes of the world's first multipurpose stadium with a retractable roof.

You'll also see a film about the architectural design of the building and take a walking tour through the dressing rooms, into a private SkyBox, and past the media centre. The real thrill for the kids though is to go down onto the field. The playing area is large enough to hold 516 African elephants. As for what holds the 112 strips of astroturf together?— 12.9 km (8 mi) of zippers. You'll be able to walk around the bases, get up close to the

KEEP IN MIND Children two and older need a ticket for the baseball games. You can buy a Family 4-Pack for about $65 that includes four baseball tickets, hot dogs, drinks, and one souvenir program. On certain days, kids can visit with the Blue Jay players before the game. And if the kids get restless? There's a supervised play area where they can let off a bit of steam before going back to their seats. A special birthday? Call ahead to have their name in lights on the Jumbo Tron.

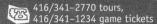 1 Blue Jays Way

Tours $12.50 adults, $8.50 youth 12–17, $7 kids 5–11

 Tours daily, except on event days. Baseball games Apr–Oct

416/341–2770 tours, 416/341–1234 game tickets

6 and up

pitching mound and visit the bullpen where the pitchers warm up. Even non-baseball fans will come away with a new appreciation of the game.

You can bring the kids here to see rock concerts and races, Pavarotti, and visiting authors such as Harry Potter's creator. It seats over 50,000 people and boasts one of the largest video display boards in the world—the Sony Jumbo Tron screen that's three-storeys high. The Toronto Argonaut football team plays here too. But mostly, you'll come to see the home games of the Toronto Blue Jays who won back-to-back World Series Championships in 1992 and 93. Would your kids like to run the bases or throw out the first pitch? On Junior Jays Saturdays (every Saturday home game), they can do both as well as be a part of the kids starting lineup for the game. Afterward, they can sit with their baseball gloves at the ready, watch the replays on the giant screen, cheer on their favourites, and wait to catch the balls that soar up into the stands.

HEY, KIDS! What exactly is a retractable roof? Like a cat that pulls in its claws, the SkyDome roof can retract its roof panels. It takes about 20 minutes and up to 750 horse-power to open. The ball players can play even in an April blizzard.

EATS FOR KIDS In the adjoining Renaissance Toronto Hotel, you can watch the game from the windows of **The Bistro** (45 Peter St. S., tel. 416/341–5045). Chef Roger makes a hearty chicken noodle soup and great fries. The chefs at **Benihana Japanese Steakhouse** (100 Front St. W., in the Fairmont Royal York Hotel, tel. 416/860–5002) cook, shake, and twirl with theatrical finesse at your table. A sports fan's mecca, **Wayne Gretzky's** (99 Blue Jays Way, tel. 416/979–PUCK) serves spicy Right Wingers (chicken wings) and Ruff & Tumble (pasta). The Great One's hockey memorabilia alone is worth the visit.

TEA AT THE FOUR SEASONS HOTEL

A re your kids' manners, or lack of manners, driving you to despair? Time for a tune-up of please and thank you and could you please pass the biscuits? Afternoon Tea at the Four Seasons Hotel in downtown Toronto is the perfect testing ground. You'll be almost guaranteed that ensconced in the casually elegant Lobby Bar, there'll be no loud burps or grunts of acknowledgement, no pushing or shoving or shouts of "He stole my cake!"

Because the hotel is home to visiting celebrities and stars, many of whom travel with baby and nanny entourage, the staff won't give you the cold shoulder when you arrive with Buster in blue jeans. They'll sit you down at a pink-tablecloth table by the window, unfold your pink napkin, pour out glasses of ice water, and start the parade of silver teapots, strainers, tiers of finger sandwiches, and cakes coming from the kitchen.

Your kids will be bowled over by the selection of goodies. A Complete Tea includes raisin scones with Devon cream as thick as cream cheese, homemade strawberry jam to slather

EATS FOR KIDS
You probably won't be hungry after all those tea goodies, but if your newly-mannered child wants dinner too, you can head upstairs to the cheerful, art-decorated **Studio Café** (tel. 416/928–7330) for a peanut butter and jam sandwich, hot dog, or pizza, lots of cheese.

HEY, KIDS!
Do you know where tea comes from? It's actually the leaves of bushes that grow in China, Japan, and Asia. If left to grow wild, they can reach up to 3 m (10 ft) high. Tea is also the most popular drink in the world. Some green teas can aid digestion and be healthy for you. It's not good to drink a lot of tea when you're young, but every now and then is OK. In some cities, you'll find people who tell your fortune after "reading" the tea leaves left in your cup. You could try it too.

on top, finger sandwiches filled with cucumber or spreads, banana bread, and fancy pastries such as lemon tarts or chocolate treats. Everyone gets their own teapot and strainer, so the junior tea drinkers will be able to pour endless cups of tea themselves and add milk and sugar, or in some cases, endless cups of milk with tea and sugar. If they don't care for strong tea, you can order a herbal cinnamon apple tea or a tea of peppermint and spearmint. And if they don't like sweets, you can order only tea.

It's a great opportunity to teach some etiquette such as you shouldn't lick the jam off the knife, or play the spoons at the table. And the kids will enjoy the ceremony of it all. Who knows? Afterward, they may even surprise you by dabbing the crumbs delicately off their mouths and asking "May I have another cup of tea, please . . .?"

KEEP IN MIND Because of Toronto's "veddy British" roots, you'll find a good cup of tea easily. At the Windsor Arms Hotel, tea is served in the city's only just-for-tea formal sitting room. In the King Edward Hotel, kids can sip up and do a thumbs-up at the portrait of the British King. To serve your own High Tea at home, visit Say Tea (2362 Bloor St. W., tel. 416/766–5425) to choose from over 125 blends, or for a Chinese experience, Ten Ren Tea & Ginseng Co. in Chinatown (454 Dundas St. W., tel. 416/598–7872).

TEXTILE MUSEUM OF CANADA

18

I f you don't know your warps from your wefts, you're all thumbs when it comes to knitting needles, or you've never been within arm's length of an exquisite Japanese wedding kimono or a hunter's robe from Mali covered with mirrors, teeth, claws, and knotted ropes, then head to the Textile Museum of Cananda. Praised as one of Toronto's best-kept secrets and the city's "best small museum," this space devoted to cloth and other materials is a good place to break when clothes shopping with the kids. Exhibits drawn from almost 9,000 artifacts, and from over 190 countries and regions, tell hundreds of fascinating stories. Who created the piece, why, and where did it come from? How did it make its way to Canada's only textile museum? And why should we bother about it today?

The constantly changing exhibits let you see something completely different each time you visit. One month it could be American quilts or Indian temple hangings. Two months later, African cottons or carpets from Afghanistan. Of particular interest to school-age kids are the collection of Chinese children's hats and the colourful hooked rugs from Newfoundland

KEEP IN MIND During holiday times and on some Wednesday evenings during July and August, the museum hosts special three-hour Fibre Focus workshops for 9- to 14-year-olds. Ask your adolescents if they would like to weave with wire mesh, make felt from wool fibres, soapy water, and a rolling pin, or create sculptures from paper pulp? If the answer's yes, call 416/599–5321, ext 2227 to see what's being offered or e-mail info@museumfortextiles.on.ca. The $15 fee includes a drink and a snack. Guided tours of the museum can also be booked by calling two weeks ahead.

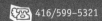

showing outport scenes. It was to this museum that Princess Diana came on a visit to sign the AIDS Quilt. The Contemporary Gallery often displays odd and intriguing things such as a hand-crocheted wallaby covered in mohair lambswool and glittery red sequins or a video from a fibre artist who mends spider webs with thread. (The spiders quickly disposed of her attempts.)

Young designers try their own textile skills in the interactive fibrespace education gallery where projects are spaced about the room. Weave with elastic strips on a loom, embroider on burlap, or learn to cast coloured yarn onto knitting needles or silk screen fabric. On Wednesday evenings and Sunday afternoons, knowledgeable volunteers assist. Weekdays, check out the small gift shop filled with unique items such as embroidered purses from India, wooly sheep from Scotland, or Raggedy Ann dolls from America.

HEY, KIDS! You probably know about polar fleece, even wear it, but do you know what is used to make it? Bet you never guessed plastic chips from your recycled pop (soda) bottles. Learn how it's done in the second-floor fibrespace education gallery.

EATS FOR KIDS There's no café in the museum but dozens of good choices are just around the corner (*see* Chinatown). Steps away are the soups and noodles of **Thai Thani** (179 Dundas St. W., tel. 416/977–4712). Another possibility is to walk over to Nathan Phillips Square (*see* Nathan Phillips Square). For a fancy dinner, try the nearby Metropolitan Hotel (110 Chestnut St.). Here **Hemispheres** (tel. 416/599-8000) offers a limited kids' menu; **Lai Wah Heen** (tel. 416/977–9899) serves excellent Cantonese food and a dim sum brunch.

TODMORDEN MILLS

The small "village" of Todmorden once housed a paper mill, grist mill, and starch factory as well as a brewery, malt house, and distillery—it was a hub of industry by the mid-1800s. Today, five structures remain including two miller's homes, among the oldest in Toronto, and a tiny 1881 railway station, moved from its original Queen Street location. The whole collection is known as the Todmorden Mills Heritage Museum and Arts Centre.

Your family can get a feel for early settler life by watching a slide show in The Brewery building—or viewing the photographs and artifacts in the small museum. Check out the children's toys. But it's more interesting to see settler life in the two homes, where costumed interpreters give guided tours. At the Terry House, a Regency cottage–like dwelling of the 1830s, kids can sweep around the kitchen fireplace, smell the chamomile plants used to brew tea, and admire a very glamourous picture of a teenage Queen Victoria in the hall. The Helliwell home of the 1860s boasts a more elegant horsehair sofa, china dolls in

KEEP IN MIND If you have nature lovers in your family, take advantage of the new Wildflower Preserve just behind the parking lot. A winding path leads past fields of wildflowers, over streams, and along a picturesque forested trail. Maintained by volunteers, the preserve changes with each season.

EATS FOR KIDS There are a few outdoor tables to picnic on adjacent to the museum. Or travel up the Pottery Road hill to the **Dairy Queen** (1040 Broadview Ave., tel. 416/425–2261) for ice-cream sundaes and a great view. On Danforth Avenue in nearby Greek Town, many restaurants welcome families with babies or toddlers. Try **Mr. Greek** (568 Danforth Ave., tel. 416/461–5470) for pitas with dip and shish kebab. Teens might enjoy **Myth** (417 Danforth Ave., tel. 416/461–8383) with its pool tables, giant TV screens, and zippy Greek fare and pizzas.

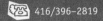
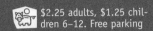
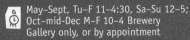

the parlour, and evening entertainments of looking at pictures through a stereoscope, a very early View-Master.

During March Break, summer Sunday afternoons, and special days such as Simcoe Day in August or Harvest Festival in September, children can partake in activities like historic cooking or papermaking. The expansive lawn is perfect for croquet or a gambol on wooden stilts. Kids will also gravitate to the back porch for old-fashioned games such as marbles or Bagatelle, an early pinball machine board that delights millennium kids as much as it did those of the past centuries.

The site itself is picturesque and there's lots of green space—9.2 hectares (28 acres)—for kids to run around. The surrounding terrain includes a wetlands, a wildflower preserve, and the beginnings of a 10-km (6-mi) hike along the Don River.

HEY, KIDS! Did you know that Toronto has its own "Leaning Tower of Pisa"? It's the chimney marked with the word "Valley" that you can see across the expressway from Todmorden. Look for the picture at the museum showing the Brick Works factory with its four chimneys, each with one word from Don Valley Brick Works. The other three are no longer standing. The Valley chimney is leaning quite a bit but people are trying to prop it up and save it.

TOMMY THOMPSON PARK

What better place to test out a new bicycle or Rollerblades than this traffic-free, 5-km (3-mi) stretch of pavement through natural wilderness just minutes from downtown? The Tommy Thompson Park, named after the city's first Commissioner of Parks and Recreation (known for his "Please Walk on the Grass" signs), encompasses wetlands, meadows, cottonwood forest, and lakeshore.

Affectionately known as the Leslie Street Spit, this recreational trail happened almost by accident. As the city developed in the late '50s, rock, gravel, sand, and concrete rubble from the extensive building was dumped onto a man-made peninsula jutting out into Lake Ontario. Within decades, the landfill site had sprouted into a green, aquatic habitat. Soon, environmental boosters were setting up basking sites for reptiles, nesting areas for turtles, underwater reefs for fish, and mudflats along the shore. Today, the park is an urban wilderness that's a bird-watchers' dream and a family escape hatch from city concrete.

HEY, KIDS! You may think that bird-watchers are funny old people dressed in hiking boots and safari hats. But kids can be bird-watchers too! See if you can spot some of the 300 kinds of birds that have been seen on the spit. Some you know like sea gulls or swans. Others have descriptive names like white-rumped sandpiper or tufted titmouse. Borrow a bird book and binoculars if you can, get a birding checklist at www.trca.on.ca, and be sure to record your sightings on the white board at the entrance to the park. See, already, you're a birder!

Energetic kids will love biking or blading the full length of the smooth roadway. At the end is a small lighthouse, but most kids come to a full stop when they reach the Spit Cart (June–Labour Day, Sa–Su 10–12) at the halfway point. There, a naturalist will let them stroke the fur of a muskrat or examine a feather, or explain the difference between frogs and toads.

As you move down the trail (or travel by shuttle bus to the 3-km [2-mi] point), you'll certainly hear birds, especially the squawks of the 40,000 to 50,000 pairs of ring-billed gulls nesting in spring, see butterflies (40 species flit about), and come upon turtles and snakes near the ponds. Watch for signs of beavers (who love chewing the cottonwood trees), wild rabbits, and swimming muskrats. You'll be lucky to glimpse a red fox or coyote or, especially in winter, a snowy owl, great-horned owl, or one of the thousands of waterfowl that don't migrate south.

GETTING THERE By car, take the Don Valley Parkway south or the Gardiner Expressway east to Lake Shore Boulevard, travel east to Leslie Street, then south half a kilometre to the entrance. By public transit, take the subway south to Queen Station, then transfer to #501 Streetcar eastbound. Get off at Jones Avenue and walk south on Leslie Street to the gates.

KEEP IN MIND There is not a lot of shade along the pathway so bring hats, sunscreen, and water for everyone. Along the way, you'll see signs for protected areas, especially in spring when birds are nesting. Careful—an angry, disturbed bird could peck at a child. Wisely, dogs are not allowed. If you make it all the way to the lighthouse, start back in good time. Although the shuttle bus (May–October every half hour) makes a final run to pick up stragglers, the parking area and main gates are locked at 6 PM.

TORONTO AEROSPACE MUSEUM

What young boy—or young girl, as an exhibit on women pilots at this museum shows—hasn't at one time dreamed of getting into the cockpit of a plane and making it fly? It's the next best thing to being Peter Pan. At the Toronto Aerospace Museum, or TAM as it's fondly known, your kids won't be able to fly. But they'll be able to see a whole range of aircraft—from tiny models in a display case to huge bombers as big as a house—and the dreams may linger still.

Because this museum devoted to local aviation history and the development of areospace is a work in progress, it's a bit like walking into somebody's project-filled workshop. You'll find bits of planes, such as the tail from a Royal Navy Nimrod sub-hunter that crashed at a Canadian National Exhibition airshow, engines used in Spitfires and Tiger Moth trainers, a repair room for damaged or new aircraft, and blueprints for a current ambitious project—a full-size replica of the ill-fated Avro Arrow that was shut down under mysterious circumstances by the Canadian government in 1959.

KEEP IN MIND Next door, Bombardier Aerospace turns out long-range jets, and turboprop regional airliners. Free tours are offered for ages 13 and up on the last Sunday of each month. If your teens are interested, call 416/373-4311 for a request form. But book ahead. They're popular.

EATS FOR KIDS There's no restaurant on site and this is definitely no picnic spot. Just south down Allen Road is the **Rainforest Cafe** in Yorkdale Shopping Centre (Highway 401 and Allen Parkway, tel. 416/780-4080). The tropical thunder and lightning and curtains of rain accompany pastas, burgers, and ice-cream desserts. Just north is **The Mandarin** (1027 Finch Ave. W., at Dufferin, tel. 416/736-6000). Even babies are welcomed by friendly waiters to the huge Chinese buffet of hot and cold dishes, including sweet-and-sour ribs, soups, and noodles.

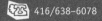
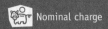

Within a former hanger where the deHavilland Aircraft of Canada company began building Tiger Moths in 1929, the display space is large enough for the huge Lancaster Mark X Bomber and a CF-5 Freedom Fighter, with room to spare for planes and propellors hanging from the ceiling. Future plans include cockpits where kids can sit and work the switches (now they can climb high stairs to peer in), aviation camps, and taxi test trials of the completed Avro Arrow.

If you have questions about some of the curiosities, such as the picture of the torturous-looking anti-gravity suit that was developed and tested by Dr. Franks and Dr. Banting (of Banting and Best fame), ask the helpful staff. They'll be glad to turn on an 18-cylinder radial engine or show you the first plane to fly like a bird, now being created by University of Toronto graduate students. But that's another dream.

HEY, KIDS! Women can be pilots too. Check out the exhibit near the front to see photos of some female fliers such as petite Eileen Vollick. A former beauty queen, she was the first woman pilot in Canada. She wore a fur-lined hooded suit to keep her warm in winter and was so small that she needed several pillows on the seat just to see out of the cockpit. In 1928 she learned how to perform airplane aerobatics and, of course, knew how to bail out of her plane in a parachute if trouble arose.

TORONTO CLIMBING ACADEMY

Look up, look way up—35 ft up to where a seven-year-old is swinging on a rope from the very top of one of Toronto Climbing Academy's climbing walls. But not to worry. She's hooked up safely with a harness and ropes to the floor below. After quickly ascending up all the hand and toe holds to the top, she'll be "belayed" back down via ropes and a pulley to ground level.

Kids seem to have an easier time than adults taking to this fast-growing sport of indoor climbing. But then, what kid doesn't love to climb? Timid ones will be content to watch. That's fine—the staff doesn't push. The owner of this 15,000-sq-ft warehouse-type space, Sasha Akalski, former coach of the Bulgarian Sports Climbing Team, believes that the focus should be on fun and, of course, safety. During the Kids Love to Climb program on Saturdays, kids learn how to put on a harness, rub their hands with a chalk ball to dry up sweat, ascend way up under the guidance of an instructor, and ride back down. Within minutes, they're asking to do it again.

EATS FOR KIDS Though this industrial area needs a clean up, good restaurants are within blocks. **The Real Jerk** (709 Queen St. E., tel. 416/463–6055) serves the city's best Jamaican food to all ages including babies in high chairs. Jerk chicken, rice, and peas are served from 1 PM on Saturdays. Teens should like the funky **Riverside Café Bistro** (730 Queen St. E., tel. 416/406–2943) with crépes and other delectables for Saturday and Sunday brunches starting at 10 AM. For early risers, **Bonjour Brioche Bakery Café** (812 Queen St. E., tel. 416/406–1250) serves eggs, croissants, and brioches from 8 AM.

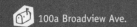 100a Broadview Ave.

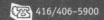 416/406-5900

 Day pass $12 adults, $10 students, $6 ages 12 and under; $35 beginner lesson ages 13 and up, Kids Love to Climb $20 ages 6–12

 Kids Love To Climb Sa 11–1; beginner lessons Tu 7, F 6:30, Sa 1, Su 12

6 and up

Teenagers can sign up for a two-hour beginner's lesson that teaches how to tie knots, secure footholds, grip crevices, and descend safely. After that, they'll be ready to use their day pass to try the more than 100 different climbs, from the beginner's walls to the medium-challenging World Cup Walls from France that replicate a wilderness rock face, to the most difficult almost upside-down climbs. A guide always works with them to "belay" them down.

Saturdays are busy with kids programs and birthday parties so you must sign up in advance. And if you would like to try climbing some of these heights along with your kids, go ahead. It gives a whole new meaning to "they're driving me up the wall."

KEEP IN MIND

Toronto Climbing Academy holds birthday parties on Saturdays and weekdays after 4:30. It's a great location as there is lots of space and picnic tables where you can serve pizza or cake. The cost: $20 per child (6 kids minimum), which includes equipment and instruction.

HEY, KIDS! You may know what a groove or a crack is and certainly you know edges. But what exactly is a gris-gris or a keeper knot? Indoor rock climbing has a whole new "lingo," or language. You'll learn about belays and bolts, hand holds and "routes." If you don't understand a term, just ask. The friendly trained staff at the Toronto Climbing Academy will be glad to explain it to you. Now how about grabs or bouldering or carabiners?

TORONTO ISLAND FERRIES

It's a treat to sail across Lake Ontario on one of the passenger ferries dating from the '30s. The gates clang shut, the ferry horn blows, and the *Thomas Rennie*, or the *Sam McBride*, pushes off on its 15-minute journey. Kids will immediately want to run up the steep flight of stairs to the open deck, with its polished wood floors, brass fittings, and see-through metal railings. Torontonians have enjoyed this scenic crossing since 1833, when a hotel on the Toronto Islands offered horse-powered ferry service to its guests.

Though most of the sights will be familiar to you—seagulls overhead and ducks in the water, sailboats, and an unencumbered view of the CN Tower—they'll be magical to a toddler or preschooler standing at the rails. "Will we hit the ducks? Hey, where did that airplane come from? Why is that police boat going so fast?" In the summer, the harbour is alive with all manner of watercraft from tour boats to tugboats, and Voyageur

EATS FOR KIDS There's no food or drink served onboard. In the waiting area, there's a snack bar and vending machines. It's best to bring your own picnic or eat first at a restaurant along Front Street like **Planet Hollywood** (227 Front St. W., tel. 416/596–7827).

HEY, KIDS! Ever since the Ojibwe First Nations canoed over to the islands for healing ceremonies, citizens have been travelling over this area of water by boat. Today, we have speedboats, yachts, sailboats, rescue craft, and water taxis. But guess what powered the very first passenger ferry over to the Islands? It was a pair of horses. The two strong animals walked continually around a turntable on the flat raft-like boat to make it move forward. You can see a picture of it in The Pier, Toronto's Waterfront Museum. That must have been some horsepower!

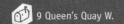 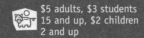 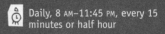

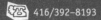 9 Queen's Quay W.

$5 adults, $3 students
15 and up, $2 children
2 and up

Daily, 8 AM–11:45 PM, every 15
minutes or half hour

416/392-8193

 10 and under

canoes from the Harbourfront summer camps. The decks are large and wide enough for kids to move around easily and wooden benches provide plenty of seating.

Ferries travel from the foot of Bay Street to three destinations—Ward's Island, Hanlan's Point, and, from spring to fall when the Centreville amusement park is open, Centre Island. You only buy one ticket and hand it in on the way over. Return is free. On a hot summer morning, there's almost a party atmosphere in the waiting area. Families carry coolers and picnic fare, sports fans are dressed for the beach volleyball courts, and tourists speaking a dozen languages line up at the gates. Nearly two million people embark on this short trip each year. From the top deck you can watch crew members throw the big ropes to pull the ferry fast, see the throngs disembark, then with another blast of the horn, you're sailing back to the opposite shore.

KEEP IN MIND To get more for your money, take the Belt Line milk-run trip operated in spring and fall after 7PM. The ferries make at least two stops along the way, so you'll get a 45-minute to one-hour trip. The view of the city is spectacular, especially at sunset or at dusk when the neon and glittering lights of the city begin to glow. And if your rollerblading superstar wants to skate back and forth on the smooth wooden decks to admire the view, sorry, no rollerblades allowed onboard or in the waiting area.

TORONTO ISLAND PARK

Ever since Toronto's first citizens rode their horses up and down the sand on the green peninsula two hundred years ago, the Toronto Islands have served as the city's playground. When a violent storm in 1858 caused the green space to separate from the mainland, the 18 small islands became even more of an urban getaway. Hotels and summer camping sites sprang up; Ferris wheels and a famous Diving Horse entertained at amusement parks. Championship sculler Ned Hanlan and baseball player Babe Ruth, who hit his first homer at the Island Stadium when he played for the Providence Grays, were among those who furthered the islands' sports and recreation allure.

The Toronto Island Park is actually 18 islets linked together by bridges. You can disembark from the ferry (*see* Toronto Island Ferries) at either end, Hanlan's Point or Ward's Island, and cycle, walk, or hop onto the trackless train (summers only) to the other islets. Along the way, you can stop off at several beaches for a swim or a volleyball game, stroll the ornamental gardens, play at the Children's Fort or the 18-hole Frisbee golf course, or detour

EATS FOR KIDS You can wander through Centreville's fast food choices (*see* Centreville Amusement Park) or head to Ward's Island where the **Rectory Café** (near ferry, tel. 416/203—6011 summers only) serves soups, salads, or chicken fajitas. For dessert, try their famous sticky buns or homemade butter tarts. The Ward's Island Café is open in summer for drinks or ice cream cones. Of course, there are dozens of picnic spots around the islands where you can throw down a blanket.

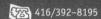 Lake Ontario

 Free

 Dawn until dark

416/392-8195

 12 and under

to Centreville Amusement Park and Far Enough Farm, (named because the parks commissioner overheard a tired mom saying to her brood, "That's it. We've walked far enough!"). From May to October, you can rent bicycles (starting from $5 an hour at Hanlan's Point or by the Lookout Pier (tel.416/203-0009) on Centre Island. None have training wheels, but two-seaters and four-seater bikes can carry those too young to ride.

Your kids may want to rent a canoe, rowboat, or pedal boat, or play hide-and-seek within the cedar hedge Maze just behind the horticultural displays on Avenue of the Islands. There's a trout pond to fish in by the 1808 Gibraltar Point Lighthouse (Toronto's oldest standing historical landmark). But you'll find the ultimate natural play space on Ward's Island where people live in cottage-style homes and the streets are car-free. Here, the beach is small and intimate, and in the spring, kids can catch tadpoles in the pond.

KEEP IN MIND

You may want to steer clear of the "Clothing Optional" a.k.a. "Nude" beach on the west side of Hanlan's Point. It's becoming a popular tourist attraction. Better to take the kids to the Centre Island beach where there are swings, volleyball nets, and a changing room.

HEY, KIDS! No one knows for sure what happened to the first lighthouse keeper, J.P. Rademuller. The story goes that ne'er-do-wells (soldiers from Fort York) looking for bootleg beer chased him up the spiral staircase of the lighthouse to the top. They knocked him out, and threw him over the edge. To hide evidence, they chopped up his body and buried the pieces over the grounds. His bones were discovered by another keeper in 1893. The next lighthouse keeper, Joe Durnan, claimed that he could hear moans and on misty nights could see Rademuller's spectre seeking his lost limbs!

TORONTO MUSIC GARDEN

This special waterfront garden owes its creation to world-famous cellist Yo-Yo Ma's love of one piece of music—the *First Suite for Unaccompanied Cello* by Johann Sebastian Bach. Ma made a video series about the piece for television in collaboration with Boston landscape designer Julie Moir Messervy. Their interpretation of the music with nature was so successful that they decided to make a permanent music garden. Plans for the location in Boston fell through, but former Toronto mayor Barbara Hall enthusiastically welcomed the idea and provided the two and a half acres just west of Harbourfront Centre.

So much the better for music lovers, green thumbs, and little explorers. Children can hide behind 5-ft ornamental grasses, play on the natural grass steps, smell the plants, and follow butterflies and perennial blossoms up a spiral path. Each of the garden's sections is named after one of the six movements of the piece. For example, the Prelude section

GETTING THERE By public transit, take the Spadina 510 streetcar south from the Spadina subway station or the LRT Harbourfront Line going west from Union Station.

EATS FOR KIDS Across the road from the Spadina Quay Wetland is **Coffee Time** (10 Lower Spadina Ave., tel. 416/260–5106), a doughnut shop serving sandwiches and hot meals such as barbecued chicken or fish. Other than that, you'll have to walk along the lake to nearby Harbourfront Centre or picnic in the garden.

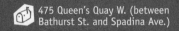 475 Queen's Quay W. (between Bathurst St. and Spadina Ave.)

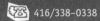 416/338-0338

 Free

 Daily

 3 and up

flows like a riverbank between granite boulders from the Canadian Shield. The Gigue, or "jig" section, presents jaunty rollicking plantings topped off with a set of large grass steps that drop you down and out of the garden. There are hiding places and open areas, birch forests, and a wrought-iron gazebo for scheduled storytelling or music performances and exuberant swing dance afternoons.

Ask for a free audio-guide with which to tour the site. The CD recording is more suited to adolescents or adults but your young ones will be able to hear parts of the inspiring piece of music and listen to Yo-Yo Ma and his collaborators talk about the garden. Children from the nearby Waterfront School contributed their impressions of the garden to the recording as well. Ma is convinced that Bach would have been delighted to stroll around the garden as happily as you and the kids.

HEY, KIDS! Yo-Yo Ma was only four years old when he learned to play a famous piece of music on his cello. This musical work had a long name— *Bach's First Suite for Unaccompanied Cello*. When Yo-Yo played the music, he saw pictures of water, air, and flowers in his mind. You might say that he was already planning this garden when he was a kid. The children who go to the public school next door get to ride their bikes or skateboard through the garden on their way to class. Lucky them!

TORONTO ON STAGE

After New York City and London, Toronto is the largest centre for English-speaking theatre in the world. You can definitely bring the kids to the big musicals such as Disney's *The Lion King* at the Princess of Wales Theatre or *Mamma Mia!* at the Royal Alexandra Theatre. But you'll also find dinner theatres, lunchtime theatres, dance theatres, summer outdoor theatres, as well as comedy shows for your sophisticated teens and an annual Christmas pantomime for your exuberant youngsters. You could find dozens of performances from sci-fi to Shakespeare in any given week.

The top tickets for the big shows are high—they can top one hundred dollars plus—but many of the smaller theatres offer pay-what-you-can matinees, preview prices, or rush seats at the last minute for about $10. You can also take advantage of the half-price tickets booth, T.O. TIX, on Level Two at the north end of the Eaton Centre. If you show up in person between noon and 7:30 on the day of performance, you can buy half-price tickets to dozens of shows that are not sold out. Some will not be suitable for kids, but many are

EATS FOR KIDS Several dinner theatres are perfect for young audiences. **Famous People Players Dinner Theatre** (110 Sudbury St., tel. 416/532–1137) offers the world-renowned black light puppet shows. **Stage West Theatre Restaurant** (5400 Dixie Rd., Mississauga, tel. 905/238–0042) often puts on musicals celebrating famous pop groups. **Medieval Times Dinner and Tournament** (Exhibition Place next to the Dufferin Gate entrance, tel. 416/260–1234) is one of Toronto's most requested tickets. Kids can cheer for the knights in the jousting tournaments while they eat roast chicken or ribs with their fingers.

 T.O. TIX booth: Level Two, Dundas Mall
Corridor, Eaton Centre, 220 Yonge Street

📞 416/536–6468 T.O. TIX

50% off ticket prices
plus small service charge

 Tu–Sa noon–7:30

2 and up

super. By showing up at noon on Saturday, you often have a good chance for Sunday shows. The ticket booth also sells advance tickets for same week performances at the world–renowned Stratford and Shaw Festivals.

Kids over seven might want to tour the Elgin and Winter Garden Theatre Centre, the last operating double-decker theatre in the world (tours Thu 5 PM, Sa 11 AM, $7 adults, $6 students). The upper theatre is painted like a garden with golden leaves hanging from the ceiling. Once a vaudeville theatre, it's now home to the raucous annual holiday pantomime where kids can shout out at over-the-top fractured fairy tales like *Robin Hood* or *Cinderella*. With free booster seats, cookies for sale during intermission, special plays just for children (*see* Young Peoples Theatre), the new Kids' Night Out program, and a high caliber of performance, the city's theatres are working hard to attract young audiences.

KEEP IN MIND

Two summer festivals are within 90 minutes drive of Toronto—the Shaw Festival in Niagara-on-the-Lake (tel. 800/511–SHAW) and the Stratford Festival (tel. 800/567–1600). Both offer family ticket prices and family-friendly Shakespeare, or plays such as *The Three Musketeers* or *Peter Pan*.

HEY, KIDS! Did you know that one of the longest-running shows in North America is in Toronto? It's *The Mousetrap* by mystery writer Agatha Christie. They have been putting it on night after night at Toronto Truck Theatre for 23 years! And people are still coming to see the famous play. It's very funny and mysterious too—you'll never guess the villain. If you'd like to take your mom or dad to see it, it's on every night but Monday. For tickets, call tel. 416/922–0084 or check out the discount ticket booth, T.O. TIX, at the Eaton Centre.

TORONTO POLICE MUSEUM

9

A re your fingerprints whirls or arches? And just who were the Dirty Tricks gang? You'll find out at the Toronto Police Museum and Discovery Centre just off the main lobby of Toronto Police Headquarters. For some kids, it's exciting (if somewhat intimidating) to walk into a building filled with uniformed officers. Often TV crews or radio reporters are here jostling for sound bytes. At other times, it's very quiet and the captain at the desk will have time to say hello.

The two-tiered museum displays a century's worth of police and crime memorabilia starting from the days of Muddy York (as Toronto was called at the end of the 19th century) when the biggest criminals were cow and horse thieves. Don't miss the 1914 paddy wagon, with its lantern lights and large padlock, at the north entrance door, or the cases of early equipment. The 1900 baton, 1905 whistle, and handcuffs seem charmingly innocent today.

EATS FOR KIDS There's definitely more than bread and water nearby. Across the street, a basement food court (777 Bay St.) offers super choices. Upstairs, **Cultures** (tel. 416/598–9501) makes bagels, soups, sandwiches, and delectable smoothies. **McDonald's** (470 Yonge St., tel. 416/922–2905) is one block north.

HEY, KIDS! It's not only men and women who work for the Toronto police force. For over one hundred years, horses such as Stormy, Trooper, and Trillium have helped the police patrol the streets. If an officer wants to work with the mounted unit, he or she must attend riding school lessons. Their horses must be black, bay, or chestnut, have a good temperament, and learn not be be bothered by sudden sights or sounds. Today, 24 horses patrol the Toronto streets. You may see some of them during parades, demonstrations, or just walking along downtown avenues.

In the museum, kids can test the interactive exhibits, such as the finger-print screener, watch a short film about an emergency call, gaze up at a mounted officer on a large horse, examine the car wreck of a drunk driver, and see the disguises (including putty for fake noses) used by the Dirty Tricks Gang. You may have trouble coaxing your kids out of the police cruiser. Buttons underneath the steering wheel flash the headlights and start the revolving beacon. Also a hit is the 1929 police station with its narrow holding cell. Behind the grilled door, wrapped in a blanket, is a shadowy figure doing time.

The museum also celebrates the city's police officers from the time they operated the first horse-drawn ambulances. Revolving uniformed mannequins, a marine officer in a boat hanging from the ceiling, and an Emergency Task Force member scaling a wall adds to the action-figure aura that surrounds officers. A poignant row of empty hats and photos honors those killed in the line of duty.

KEEP IN MIND There's much information here, some of which may not be suitable for youngsters. Do you really want to explain the Elonzo Boyd gang who used a dummy head for target practice, or the rapist who strangled his victim with an iron cord? Some of the crimes are pretty gruesome, even for adults, so you may want to brush past the exhibit cases and stick to visiting the holding cell, admiring the Mountie's lifesize horse, and flashing the lights in the police cruiser. On the other hand, it's a good opportunity to discuss crime and punishment, especially with teens.

TORONTO ZOO

When the Toronto Zoo first opened in 1974, it was considered revolutionary—no creatures in small cages, an animal nutritionist on staff, and some 710 acres (287 hectares) of space. People used to "doing the zoo" in one hour complained. But since then, this zoo, the third largest in the world, has set a standard for promoting conservation, encouraging natural behaviours, and undertaking the research to produce babies of endangered species—lots of babies. Some 73 wood bison have been bred and reintroduced to the Canadian north, 15,000 Puerto Rican Crested Toads have been hatched and released, and the cheetahs have produced nine babies in 10 years. In 1999 the zoo celebrated its 25th birthday by making cakes for the animals. What kind of cake for a gorilla? A concoction of gelatin, fruit, vegetables, and whipped cream. Recently two baby giraffes, two lion cubs and two orphaned polar bear cubs were welcomed to the fold.

The Zoo is arranged in six bio-geographical regions so you can travel to Africa, Australasia, Eurasia, the Americas, IndoMalaya, and Canada—but not all in one day. If

HEY, KIDS! With some 5,000 animals and 250 exhibits, you can't possibly see every fuzzy or slimy creature in one visit. Check the "Today's Zoo News" whiteboard outside the ticket booth to see when the feedings and "Meet the Keeper" events take place. And be sure to pick up a zoo guide at the Main Entrance. Once inside, you can follow the coloured animal footprints. Would you like to take the one-hour Grizzly Bear Trail? Or, if you're feeling really energetic, the three-hour Round the World Tour?

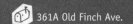
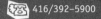
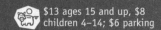
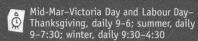

you have small children, you may want to detour to the Children's Area near the main gate where they can ride a pony or camel, or play at the children's playground. The open-air Zoomobiles ($3) constantly cruise the grounds but if you want to see a lot of animals, some walking is required.

What will your kids beg to go back to? The Edge of Night, a dark pavilion where you can see nocturnal animals in action, and of course, the busy apes who are hilarious to watch in their new rainforest home. Top ape for smarts is gorilla Josephine, who has produced nine babies with the magnificent silver-back Charles. Also a hit with kids are the polar bears and the underwater viewing area where you can watch these strong swimmers.

GETTING THERE Take the Don Valley Parkway north to Hwy 401 east. Take exit 389 at Meadowvale Rd. and drive one mile north to the zoo. Look for the zoo signs—the way is well marked. By transit, take the Bloor subway east to Kennedy Station and transfer to Bus 86A, which stops at the zoo gates.

KEEP IN MIND During summer, it's best to arrive early before all the animals are sleeping in the heat; the zoo generally starts letting people in around 8:50 AM. Because many Canada Geese are present, there are a lot of droppings. Everyone should wear shoes that can be easily cleaned. If your little ones tire easily, rent a stroller or a wagon at the entrance. Wheelchairs are free. The Family Centre adjacent to the African Pavilion has changing rooms and a nursing station. Bottle warming is provided at any restaurant.

TORONTO'S FIRST POST OFFICE

If quill pens, ink pots, sealing wax, and sand seem archaic to parents, imagine how ancient these tools must seem to kids who send e-mail messages in an instant. Yet it's still a kick for kids to write a letter the old-fashioned way. At Toronto's first post office, set up by the British postmaster in 1833 and still operating as a Canada Post postal station, children can not only try writing with bird feathers dipped into ink, but they can seal the folded papers with melted wax and post their letter to anywhere in the world.

Sundays are good days for families to visit, when the costumed postmistress sits behind the postal counter to explain how people knew that mail had arrived (the postmaster published it in the newspaper) or how long a letter took to cross the ocean (about two months). But arrive on any day of the week to see the permanent exhibit, Royal Mail—Postal Service 1830–1840, displaying early letters and coins, or to have the curator

KEEP IN MIND

Although the post office uses Sheaffer's ink rather than the pigment ink dyes of the period, your junior scribbler's fingers may become quite inky. Try washing the stains off with warm water and lemon juice.

EATS FOR KIDS **Siegfried's Dining Room** (300 Adelaide St. E., tel. 416/415–2260) at George Brown College next door serves lunches, but call ahead in case the college is not in session. Or walk down Frederick Street to the **Patrician Grill** (219 King St. E., tel. 416/366–4841), an old-fashioned diner-style restaurant that's a Toronto institution. You could also picnic in the St. James Cathedral gardens (65 Church St., tel. 416/364–7865) with fixings like a peameal bacon sandwich from the **Carousel Bakery** (93 Front St. E., tel. 416/363–4247) at the St. Lawrence Market.

 260 Adelaide St. E.

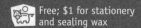 Free; $1 for stationery and sealing wax

 M–F 9–4, Sa–Su 10–4

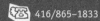 416/865–1833

 8 and up

help you write an old-fashioned letter in the cosy Reading Room. Here, citizens once read their mail by the fire or wrote return correspondence. Ask to see the pickwick. The unusual object picks the wick out of the beeswax coated candle so you can melt the wax onto an envelope and stamp it with a tiny seal of a cat, or for secret messages, a seal with "Entre Nous" (Between Us) etched above a miniature envelope.

In the back room, a model of old Toronto sits under a replica of Upper Canada's first stamp— a beaver. Afterward you can buy seals as well as postcards, wax, ink, and Canadian, British, and American stamps at the postal counter. But the real thrill is to watch your sealed letter stamped with the original "York-Toronto 1833" and "City of Toronto, U.C." cancellations and sent to any corner of the globe. You could even post it to yourself as a souvenir.

HEY, KIDS! The quill pens in the pot on the writing table are bird feathers, cleaned and cut with a special knife. But these quills were not plucked from the birds. A certain number of feathers fall off naturally each year. Try the striped feather from a wild turkey or the black feather from a Canada goose. A crow feather is good for fine writing, but to look very elegant, a lady might have chosen the kind of white swan feather on display. It was this kind of quill pen that was used to sign the American Declaration of Independence.

THE WATERFRONT TRAIL

In 1995 Toronto was named North America's best cycling city by *Bicycling Magazine*—and who's going to argue with them? Join the hundreds who are helmeting up and pedaling across the over 125 km (78 mi) of trails crisscrossing the city—through ravines, around the islands, and along Toronto's streets. Probably one of the best paths for families is the 22-km (14-mi) Waterfront Trail (also known as the Martin Goodman Trail after a former *Toronto Star* president). It runs from east to west along the Lake Ontario shore. There are no hills, just scenery, and many things to view along the way if you want a sightseeing break. If you're really energetic, you could bike to other safe bicycle paths on the Leslie Street Spit (weekends only), the Islands, or High Park.

Start at the foot of Silver Birch Avenue in the family-friendly Beaches, where the trail begins alongside the beach boardwalk. If fatigue sets in, you can stop at one of the two large playgrounds or have a swim at the Donald Summerville Olympic Pools before continuing out to Ashbridge's Bay Park. Follow the squiggly blue and green lines marking the trail

KEEP IN MIND If you haven't been on a bicycle since you were about as high as one, don't worry. CAN-BIKE teaches the bicycle basics for kids and adults (tel. 416/392–1311). A 12-hour course for kids 9–12 covers road hazards, signalling, changing gears—all you need to know about cycling—for about $50. The Adult Learn to Ride courses start with the basics—how to balance, stop, and start.

 From the Eastern Beaches
to the Western Beaches

 Free

 24 hours

 416/943–8080

 4 and up

over the shipping canal and through the Port Lands to downtown. You'll cycle by some of Toronto's major attractions—Harbourfront Centre, the SkyDome and the CN Tower, Fort York, and Ontario Place where the trail takes you right past the box office for the Cinesphere theatre. You could stop to see an IMAX movie on the gigantic screen.

Farther west, you'll be coasting past beaches again to Marilyn Bell Park, who made headlines when she swam across Lake Ontario at the age of 16. The kids will also be interested in hearing about Sunnyside—you'll cycle past the 1922 Bathing Pavilion. The good news is that if your junior cyclist just can't take any more pedaling, you can take your bikes onto all TTC vehicles—buses, streetcars, and subways except during peak rush hours (6:30–9:30 AM and 3:30–6:30 PM). No matter how far you get, it'll be an easy ride back home.

HEY, KIDS! By law, cyclists under 18 must wear a helmet and have a bicycle bell. If you're caught without them, it's a $65 fine. It's also practical to carry water and a whistle for loud traffic areas. At night, remember your lights and reflector tape.

EATS FOR KIDS An obvious place to stop is the roughly half-way point at Harbourfront Centre where you can sit at an outdoor table at **Spinnakers** (207 Queen's Quay W., tel. 416/203–0559) or **Lakeside EATS** at Harbourfront (tel. 416/973–4600) and watch your bikes. There are all kinds of picnicking places along the way including the Eastern and Western Beaches, the Toronto Islands, the Tommy Thompson Park (weekends only), or High Park. A true moveable feast.

THE WAVE POOL

Calling all little fishes. The Lois Hancey Aquatic Centre, otherwise known as the Richmond Hill Wave Pool, is a state-of-the-art pool. You won't find the usual rectangular pool in a dark recreation centre reeking of chlorine here. This L-shaped pool has a sweeping painted shore, two-storey floor-to-ceiling windows, fake palm trees, patio umbrellas, and goofy papier mâché fish and sea creatures hanging from the ceiling. It's light and bright—just like a beach. No wonder the pool has won an outstanding attraction award. All that's missing is the sand.

Little ones can play at the edge of the gradually sloping "shore" (the deep end is 2.4 m/ 8 ft). When the waves come on strong at the other end (every 15 minutes), it creates a lapping effect in the shallow end. Tots can jump in the small swells or ride a flutter board in the white caps. Toys such as beach balls and life jackets in all sizes, even adult, are free. The wave intervals last 15 minutes and there's a break in between. (There are hours for leisure swims, when people use the pool for laps and there are no waves.)

HEY, KIDS!
You can ride the high waves or use the big slide. But you must be able to swim at least 5 m (17 ft) on your own. The lifeguards dressed in the blue and yellow uniforms will test you. Or, you can show them your Aqua Five–level certificate.

KEEP IN MIND Not only can you schedule birthday parties at the Wave Pool but you can book the entire pool for family reunions or large parties. The birthday party packages include invitations for 10, swimming during wave ($94) or leisure times ($77), use of a party room for one hour, place settings, and a party host. To rent the entire pool, and what fun that would be, it's $154 per hour for up to 100 people for waves and from $138 for leisure. If you want the viewing gallery for drinks and food, it's an extra $75. Booking times are mostly in the evenings.

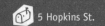 5 Hopkins St.

 Wave swim $5.50 ages 16 and up, $3 ages 3–15; Leisure swim $2.75 ages 16 and up, $1.75 ages 3–15

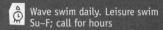 Wave swim daily. Leisure swim Su–F; call for hours

 905/508-9283

1–11

Your older ones will head straight to the twisting orange 49-m (160-ft) water slide or grab a mat or water noodle and swim to the corner of the pool where the waves are strongest. As the waves go up and down, the kiddie-beach set lying on its coloured mats ooh and aah. Meanwhile, you can relax in the large swirl pool, a whirlpool that's kept at 95°F, or relax in the sauna off the pool deck.

If your kids are under eight years old, a parent or guardian at least 16 years old must be within arm's length. If they're preteen and you don't want to get wet, you can watch them from a large viewing gallery upstairs that overlooks the pool. Do you have children with special needs? No problem. The fully accessible changing rooms and the pool equipped with ramps and chairs means everyone will have a whale of a time.

EATS FOR KIDS Along Yonge Street just south is every fast-food joint you can imagine but if you want sit-down family friendliness, there's **East Side Mario's** (10520 Yonge St., tel. 905/770–4000) six lights north of Major Mackenzie Drive. The Italian eatery serves activity packs along with the pizza or burger kids' meals. Dessert is extra but the menu arrives in a View-Master. A picture's worth a thousand words. **Mr. Greek** (9218 Yonge St., tel. 905/709–9800) offers full platters of shish kebabs or roast chicken with feta cheese salads.

WILD WATER KINGDOM

4

Your water babies, water nymphs, and water rats will love getting soaked at Canada's largest water park. Even so, if your family is in the habit of plunging down water slides at the biggest parks on the Continent, you'll find Wild Water Kingdom a bit tame. On the other hand, there are enough water slides, speed slides, tube slides, pools, and interactive water activities to keep everyone happy. And the park is small enough to keep track of your sea serpents and mermaids.

For the brave of heart and those over 48 inches, the most exciting thrills come from White Lightning and The Cliff, the two seven-storey speed slides. Other free-fall rides include the Devil's Drop, four shotgun slides into an 2.5-m (8-ft) pool (for strong swimmers only), and the Little Twister and the Cork Screw slides. Need a time-out? Relax in one of the large, family hot tubs or bob around the Lazy River circuit on an inner tube for a quarter mile. Life preservers are free of charge for little ones who want to join mom

KEEP IN MIND There's not much shade in the park so sunscreen is essential. Bring water—to drink—to prevent dehydration. If it's hot and sunny, bring hats for between slide sunning. This is not the place to insist on good nutrition as there's little alternative to fast-food options. If you want to avoid the Pogo dogs, fries with gravy and cheese curds, and Philly Steak sandwiches, bring a picnic and head for the tables under the trees.

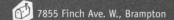 7855 Finch Ave. W., Brampton

 $19.95 ages 10 and up, $15.50 ages 4–9; some activities extra

 June, Sa–Su 10–6, July–mid-Aug, daily 10–8, mid-Aug–early Sept, daily 10–6

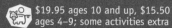 905/794–0565 or 416/369–0123 (recorded message)

 2 and up

and dad in the Tidal Wave Pool. And for kids who just can't wait in line, you can rent a tube for the day. Dolphin Bay is an interactive play area where kids about six and under (under 54 inches) shoot water pumps, shower under water curtains, slide down a green frog's tongue, and ride pink tubes across a small incline.

When your kids are completely water-soaked, head for the two 18-hole mini-golf courses, the bumper boats, professional batting cages, the games arcade, or the Children's Adventure Playground (good for preschoolers). The best feature about the park is that it borders 100 acres of lawns, trees, and a lake offering green space for picnicking, volleyball games, or pedaling around on a pedal boat. On the wide open space under the trees, you can barbecue hot dogs, toss a Frisbee, inspect the bulrushes, or just try to get dry from all that H_2O.

HEY, KIDS! Shivering because you've been in the water too long? Your brain is sending signals to your muscles that you're cold. And shivers are your body's effort to produce heat to warm you up. Help your body out by wrapping it in a towel or sweater, and parking it in the sun.

GETTING THERE By car, take the Gardiner Expressway to the QEW (Queen Elizabeth Way) west. Follow signs for Highway 427 north and follow past the airport to the Finch Avenue cutoff. Take Finch West and follow the signs for about 2 km (1.2 mi) to the park. By transit, take the subway to either Yorkdale or York Mills station, then board the GO bus to the park.

WOODBINE RACE TRACK

Y̶ou might think that the race track is the last place for children. Visions of down-and-outers betting their last cent in a murky, smoke-filled arena? Well you haven't been to Woodbine Race Track, a colour-filled, spanking-clean facility near the airport. Yes, there is a slots casino here. But it's totally separate from where you'll be, viewing the horses and the jockeys in their silks in the paddock ring, or watching the races by the rails or from the stands. This race track sponsors family days, a children's area for crafts and games, and back-stretch tours. You'll find magicians and clowns and even Sno-Cone days. Bugles sound, airplanes fly overhead, the crowd cheers or wails. And even if your family doesn't win its fortunes, it's an outing that should cost you less than a visit to a theme park or a ball game, even if you bet on every race.

KEEP IN MIND Legally, those 18 and under can't bet in Ontario. But you can take your child's picks and bet for them. If you win, I'm sure you'll share some of the winnings with your junior racing consultants. After all, pari-mutuel betting means "to bet amongst us."

The best way to start a visit is to pick up the $2.50 daily program and ask for the free *Betting for Beginners* brochure from one of the many customer service reps scattered

EATS FOR KIDS The favourite for families is **Favourites** (416/675–7223), a two-tiered restaurant overlooking the track with both buffet and à la carte dining . The new **Food Court** on the second floor serves up fried chicken, pizza, meatloaf, chili, or sausage in a bun. Sit at a table or take your finger foods outside to the stands. For a real splurge, non-members can book a table at the **Woodbine Club** (416/675–7223) where the racehorse owners, trainers, and horsey set hang out. It's $20 per person plus $31 for a sumptuous buffet. And yes, the betting window here takes $2 bets.

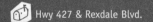 Hwy 427 & Rexdale Blvd.

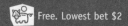 Free. Lowest bet $2

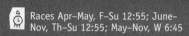 Races Apr–May, F–Su 12:55; June–Nov, Th–Su 12:55; May–Nov, W 6:45

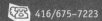 416/675-7223

 6 and up

about the building. It's everything you ever wanted to know about racing from how to read the fine print to how the odds work or what to say at the ticket window. It's also a good opportunity to give your school-age kids a little reading or math practice. They can figure out the odds with a $2 bet by using an easy equation: 10 to 1 odds equals 10 over 1 times 2 plus 2. Your $2 bet would win you $22 if your horse won.

The Woodbine Race Track is the Continent's largest racing facility and home to the oldest continuing stakes event (the Queen's Plate). You'll see a statue of the famous Canadian racehorse Northern Dancer at the entrance. Despite the prestige of the Queen's Plate and other races, you might encounter hooked-on gamblers who are sadly betting away their wages. Take this opportunity to have a frank discussion with your teens about gambling and addiction in general and ask how they would deal with it.

HEY, KIDS! What's the best way to pick a good horse? Some like the way a horse looks. Some pick because of the colours on a jockey's silks. Maybe you like an unusual name like "Rock the Clock." You can look in the program for the odds-on horse most likely to win but remember, favourites don't always come through. Sometimes a long shot, a horse who has no history of winning, surges ahead of the pack to win. That's when it's really exciting for horse, jockey, owner, trainer, and those who bet on the long shot.

YORK-DURHAM HERITAGE RAILWAY

When a diesel engine arrives—with bells clanging, whistle blowing, and smoke puffing out the smokestack—everyone stops to look, children and adults alike. Especially when it's a 1951 engine pulling cars that date from the 1920s. You can take a "Trip to Yesterday," as your train ticket boasts on this York-Durham Heritage Railway, and choose between the 1924 coach with its blue benches or the cosy 1954 car with maroon upholstered seats. As the train sets off from the Whitchurch-Stouffville Station for the hour-long 20-km (12.4-mi) ride to Uxbridge, you'll be travelling along the same rail route that once carried ice from Lake Simcoe to the ice boxes of Toronto citizens.

Kids can pick up a free colouring book at the gift shop counter in the first car. But once rolling, they'll be waiting for the high-sounding train whistle at each crossing and waving to people along the route. For a better view of the passing landscape, walk them to the baggage car where there's an open fenced observation gate. As you rumble along the Oak

HEY, KIDS! Ask the conductor or the trainmen any question you like. They will tell you when the train is about to sound the two long whistles followed by one short and one long (it happens at each railroad crossing), where you can see a beaver dam, and how many timber wolves have been spotted alongside the track—two. Keep your eyes open for deer, birds, and other wildlife. The beavers will probably be asleep in their lodge after all that hard work cutting down trees.

 Main St., Stouffville

 905/852–3696

 $17 ages 13 and up,
$9 children 4–12;
one-way fares available.
Some rides extra

 Early June–mid-Oct, Sa–Su,
depart Stouffville 1, 4, depart
Uxbridge 11, 2:30

2 and up

Ridges Moraine, a narrow ridge of high land formed during the last great ice age, you'll climb up to 351 m (1,152 ft) above sea level. Along the way, you'll pass a gravel pit, ride through a golf course (watch for stray balls), and see the areas fighting off housing development as well as experience groves of evergreens, wetlands, and rolling hills where wildlife roam.

Once you've arrived at the restored historic 1904 Uxbridge train station for the half-hour stop, visit the small museum showing conductor's hats and old luggage, and the elegant women's and children's waiting room under the eye of Queen Victoria and Prince Albert. Come back in time to watch the diesel engine travel down the track to be hooked up again to the front of the train. Some will have to cover their ears while others will love the noisy clanging and chuffing. Before you know it, it's "All Aboard" for the ride back.

GETTING THERE Follow the Don Valley Parkway north to the Stouffville Side Road. Drive east and continue until you reach the town of Stouffville. The new railway station is on the north side of Main Street, right beside the tracks, of course.

KEEP IN MIND There's no extra charge for birthdays onboard. In fact, there's a 5% discount for 20 people. Of course, you bring the food, decorations, and onboard entertainment. You can board the train at either the Uxbridge Station (a longer drive from Toronto but more to see in town) or the Whitchurch-Stouffville Station where the GO train leaves every day for Toronto. Special-event trains include the Spooky Halloween trips and a Christmas Santa run, weather permitting.

YOUNG PEOPLES THEATRE

Young Peoples Theatre, or YPT, is known for its innovative and award-winning presentations for kids. Believing that theatre should be a part of every child's life, the theatre's artistic directors have consistently presented high-quality shows at an affordable price. Every production has scheduled pay-what-you-can performances; tickets start selling at 10 AM the day of the show.

An annual season includes from five to eight plays, some geared to younger audiences such as a black-light puppet version of the popular *The Very Hungry Caterpillar* and *The Very Quiet Cricket*, and others for older kids or teens. It could be a ribald romp like *The Complete Works of William Shakespeare (abridged)* or an interpretation of *The Diary of Anne Frank*. Whatever the play, you'll find high-caliber staging, costumes, musical accompaniment, and professional actors like Brent Carver, who played in *The Prisoner of Zenda* here and went on to star at the Stratford Festival and win a Tony on Broadway.

KEEP IN MIND YPT's presentations are geared to ages 4 and up. If you want to introduce a wiggly two-year-old to the theatre, try the Solar Stage Kids' Theatre (tel. 416/368–8031) in North York. Its Sunday shows about Snow White or teddy bears will delight the very young.

EATS FOR KIDS Because the theatre is within walking distance of the market area, there are lots of choices for pre- or post-theatre family dining. Good choices very close by include **On the Rocks** (169 Front St. E., tel. 416/862–2901), a small restaurant almost next door serving excellent Chinese, Szechuan, and Cantonese lunches and dinners, or **Zoulpy's Deli Restaurant** (244 King St. E., tel. 416/594–3737), offering fish and chips and great burgers. Drinks and cookies are for sale in the theatre both before and after the shows.

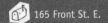 165 Front St. E.

 416/363–5131,
416/862–2222 tickets

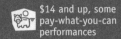 $14 and up, some
pay-what-you-can
performances

  Oct–May

 4 and up

What you won't find in either the 468-seat theatre or the 115-seat studio is an old rehash of a tired drama. Take for example, *Mella Mella*, an African folktale about a village medicine woman who holds very special powers and a young girl's quest to save her father's life and her village. The costumes, instruments, masks, and melodies straight from West Africa delighted the audience. The author went on to win an outstanding playwright award. A world away you might say from your average kiddie production!

Besides offering school productions, a renowned drama school, teachers' study guides, and over 100 public performances each year, YPT also hosts birthday parties either before or after the show. From the costumes on display in the front windows to the whimsical sets on stage, the theatre's warm and friendly environment inspires an appreciation of the arts. If the theatre keeps winning awards, it's because these kid-oriented productions are as good as or better than the adult productions in town.

HEY, KIDS! Did you know that this building used to be a stable? It was home to the 500 horses who pulled the streetcars in Toronto. You can still see the old stable arches in the basement by the washroom. Then the building became an electric generating plant. When the company started getting power from Niagara Falls, the building was going to be torn down. Canadian actress Susan Rubes thought it would be a good place for kids to see theatre. Aren't you glad she and others fought for a children's theatre?

extra! extra!

THE CLASSICS

"I'M THINKING OF AN ANIMAL..." With older kids you can play 20 Questions: Have your leader think of an animal, vegetable, or mineral (or, alternatively, a person, place, or thing) and let everybody else try to guess what it is. The correct guesser takes over as leader. If no one figures out the secret within 20 questions, the first person goes again. With younger children, limit the guessing to animals and don't put a ceiling on how many questions can be asked. With rivalrous siblings, just take turns being leader. Make the game's theme things you expect to see at your day's destination.

"I SEE SOMETHING YOU DON'T SEE AND IT IS BLUE." Stuck for a way to get your youngsters to settle down in a museum? Sit them down on a bench in the middle of a room and play this vintage favorite. The leader gives just one clue—the colour—and everybody guesses away.

FUN WITH THE ALPHABET

"I'M GOING TO THE GROCERY..." The first player begins, "I'm going to the grocery and I'm going to buy... " and finishes the sentence with the name of an object, found in grocery stores, that begins with the letter "A." The second player repeats what the first player has said, and adds the name of another item that starts with "B." The third player repeats everything that has been said so far and adds something that begins with "C" and so on through the alphabet. Anyone who skips or misremembers an item is out (or decide up front that you'll give hints to all who need 'em). You can modify the theme depending on where you're going that day, as "I'm going to X and I'm going to see..."

"I'M GOING TO ASIA ON AN ANT TO ACT UP." Working their way through the alphabet, players concoct silly sentences stating where they're going, how they're traveling, and what they'll do.

FAMILY ARK   Noah had his ark—here's your chance to build your own. It's easy: Just start naming animals and work your way through the alphabet, from antelope to zebra.

WHAT I SEE, FROM A TO Z   In this game, kids look for objects in alphabetical order—first something whose name begins with "A," next an item whose name begins with "B," and so on. If you're in the car, have children do their spotting through their own window. Whoever gets to Z first wins. Or have each child play to beat his own time. Try this one as you make your way through zoos and museums, too.

PLAY WHILE YOU WAIT

NOT THE GOOFY GAME Have one child name a category. (Some ideas: first names, last names, animals, countries, friends, feelings, foods, hot or cold things, clothing.) Then take turns naming things that fall into that category. You're out if you name something that doesn't belong in the category—or if you can't think of another item to name. When only one person remains, start again. Choose categories depending on where you're going or where you've been—historic topics if you've seen a historic sight, animal topics before or after the zoo, upside-down things if you've been to the circus, and so on. Make the game harder by choosing category items in A-B-C order.

DRUTHERS How do your kids really feel about things? Just ask. "Would you rather eat worms or hamburgers? Hamburgers or candy?" Choose serious and silly topics—and have fun!

BUILD A STORY "Once upon a time there lived..." Finish the sentence and ask the rest of your family, one at a time, to add another sentence or two. Bring a tape recorder along to record the narrative—and you can enjoy your creation again and again.

GOOD TIMES GALORE

WIGGLE & GIGGLE   Give your kids a chance to stick out their tongues at you. Start by making a face, then have the next person imitate you and add a gesture of his own—snapping fingers, winking, clapping, sneezing, or the like. The next person mimics the first two and adds a third gesture, and so on.

JUNIOR OPERA   During a designated period of time, have your kids sing everything they want to say.

THE QUIET GAME   Need a good giggle—or a moment of calm to figure out your route? The driver sets a time limit and everybody must be silent. The last person to make a sound wins.

THE A-LIST

BEST IN TOWN
CN Tower
Royal Ontario Museum
Ontario Science Centre
Harbourfront Centre
Toronto Islands

BEST OUTDOORS
The Kortright Centre for Conservation

BEST CULTURAL ACTIVITY
Young Peoples Theatre (or Hockey Hall of Fame and Museum,
depending on how you define culture)

BEST MUSEUM
The Royal Ontario Museum

WACKIEST
Casa Loma

NEW & NOTEWORTHY
Toronto Music Garden

SOMETHING FOR EVERYONE

MANY THANKS!

This book would never have been completed without help from some special people. Kudos to my parents Philip and Jasmine Pocock, who took their seven kids gallivanting over land and sea to foster a sense of adventure and a taste for travel. To the tourism folks who provided support and ideas—Tom Boyd and Helen Lovekin of Ontario Tourism and Tricia Hosking of Tourism Toronto—many thanks. Also, much appreciation to all 68 attractions for answering questions, giving tours and interviews, and being just as enthusiastic as I about the book. I'm also very grateful to my good-humored fact-checkers Hailey Biback, Molly Hoskins, and Mary Pocock and to my thumbs-up Toronto testers, Jessica and Tim Whitney. Many thanks too to editor Christina Knight at Fodor's. Finally, thanks to my husband Glenn, who provided humour, encouragement, chauffeuring services, and fast-food suppers on many nights, and to my three children Will, Dustin, and Natalie, my fearless travel companions and critics, who have taught me for the last 20 years to see the world through different eyes, you are the best!

–Kate Pocock